S0-AFO-046

Irish
Castles

TERENCE REEVES-SMYTH

APPLETREE GUIDE

Published by
Appletree Press Ltd
The Old Potato Station
14 Howard Street South
Belfast BT7 1AP
Tel: +44 (0) 28 90 243074
Fax: +44 (0) 28 90 246756
Web site: www.appletree.ie
Email: reception@appletree.ie

© Terence Reeves-Smyth, 1995

All rights reserved. Printed in India. No part of this
publication may be reproduced or transmitted in
any form or by any means, electronic or mechanical,
photocopying, recording or in any information
or retrieval system without prior permission
in writing from the publisher.

A catalogue record for this publication
is available from the British Library.

ISBN 0 86281 449 9

9 8 7 6 5 4 3 2

Picture Acknowledgements

Dr. A.S.K. Abraham: page 75
HMSO (Department of the Environment,
Northern Ireland): pages 7, 8, 30, 32, 45, 47, 90
Paul McCooey: pages 19, 85
Ken and Marie Neill: pages 15, 17, 65, 80, 82
J. Pim: page 76
Alice Reeves-Smyth: pages 40, 41, 74
Anne Reeves-Smyth: pages 37, 93
Sheila Reeves-Smyth: page 10

CONTENTS

INTRODUCTION

Ireland is a land of castles. Many hundreds lie scattered throughout the country and these, large and small, remain a striking and very visible manifestation of the social and military demands of Ireland's medieval landed classes. The earliest fortified residences – as castles may be defined – were built by the Anglo-Normans to consolidate their hold on conquered territories; many were large constructions, reflecting the enormous wealth and power that some of the barons had acquired. However, with the collapse of central authority in the fourteenth century and the resurgence of Gaelic chiefs, the size of castles diminished, while their numbers increased dramatically as every landed gentleman now needed a stronghouse for his own security. Consequently, one of the most ubiquitous monuments of the Irish countryside are the tower houses that the minor gentry built for themselves from 1400 until 1640. The wide use of artillery during the 1641 Rebellion made castles redundant, though this did not prevent Parliamentary troops from systematically slighting huge numbers of castles in the 1650s. Indeed, it seems that most Irish castles may be counted among – to use Marie Lloyd's phrase – "the ruins that Cromwell knocked about a bit".

This book is designed to provide information on a selection of Irish castles that are accessible to the public. Every effort has been made to provide a representative selection, though inevitably the choice reflects both personal taste and the constraints of the book. Many of those included are in good condition and well presented to the public, but visitors are warned that there are others in a dangerous condition, which should be explored with care and which are unsuitable for children. It should not be assumed that castles in state care are safe, though most are less dangerous and more accessible than those in private ownership.

The castles in this book are arranged alphabetically on an all-Ireland county basis. Opening times and other practical details are given at the end of each entry, as well as the National Grid Reference (NGR). Visitors should appreciate that the names of keyholders are always liable to change. Further information about castles worth visiting may be obtained in the book *Castles and Stronghouses of Ireland* by Mike Salter (Folly Publications, 1993). The best general account of the subject is Harold Leask's *Irish Castles and Castellated Houses*, published in 1941 but still available in reprint.

CARRICKFERGUS CASTLE

County Antrim

The mighty stronghold of Carrickfergus, once the centre of Anglo-Norman power in Ulster, is a remarkably complete and well-preserved early medieval castle that has survived intact despite 750 years of continuous military occupation. From its strategic position on a rocky promontory, originally almost surrounded by sea, the castle commanded Belfast Lough, and the land approaches into the walled town that developed beneath its shadow.

The core of the castle – the inner ward and keep – was built by John de Courcy, who conquered east Ulster in 1177 and ruled as a petty king until 1204, when he was ousted by another Norman adventurer, Hugh de Lacy. Initially de Courcy built the inner ward, a small bailey at the end of the promontory with a high polygonal curtain wall and east gate. It had a number of buildings, including a great hall, and must have been very cramped, especially after the keep was built in the north corner.

Probably built in the late 1180s, the keep is a massive four-storey tower, 90-feet high, with a second-storey entrance. Its entry chamber, originally one large, poorly lit room with a double latrine and no fireplace, served as the public room. A shaft gave access to a well below and a mural stair led down to the vaulted storage cellar. De Courcy's curia probably used the third storey, another poorly lit room, with a fireplace and a single latrine. The fourth storey, a high, brightly lit room with windows in all four walls, a fireplace and single latrine, was the principal chamber and must have served as de Courcy's private quarters.

Following its capture by King John in 1210, the castle passed to the crown, and constables were appointed to command the place. In 1217 the constable, De Serlande, was assigned £100 to build a new curtain wall so that the approach along the rock could be protected, as well as the eastern approaches over the sand exposed at low tide. This middle-ward curtain wall was later reduced to ground level in the eighteenth century, save along the seaward side, where it survives with a postern gate and the east tower – notable for a fine array of cross-bow loops at basement level.

After being restored to the Ulster Earldom in 1227, Hugh de Lacy returned to Carrickfergus, where he remained until his death in 1242. It was almost certainly de Lacy who enclosed the remainder of the promontory to form an outer ward, doubling the area of the castle. Its curtain wall follows the line of the rock below, with two

Carrickfergus Castle

polygonal towers on the west and an impressive gatehouse with twin flanking towers on the north. Both towers were originally circular in plan, like the contemporary gatehouse at Chepstow in Gwent, but during the sixteenth century were cut in half and lowered in height to accommodate artillery. A chamber on the first floor of the east tower is believed to have been the castle's chapel on account of its fine Romanesque-style double window surround, though the original chapel must have been in the inner ward. The ribbed vault over the entrance passage, the murder hole and the massive portcullis at either end of the gatehouse are later insertions, probably part of the remodelling that followed Edward Bruce's long and bitter siege of 1315-16.

After the collapse of the Earldom of Ulster in 1333, the castle remained the Crown's principal residential and administrative centre in the North. During the sixteenth and seventeenth centuries a number of improvements were made to accommodate artillery, notably externally splayed gunports and embrasures for cannon, though these improvements did not prevent the castle from being attacked and captured on many occasions during this time. When General Schomberg besieged and took the castle in 1690, its importance was already in decline. In 1760 it was captured and held by French invaders under the command of Thurot. Later it served as a prison and during the Napoleonic Wars was heavily defended; six guns on the east battery remain of the twenty-two that were used in 1811. For a century it remained a magazine and armoury before being transferred to the Government in 1928 for preservation as an ancient monument.

Located on the sea front beside the Marine Highway. NGR: J 415873. State Care Monument. Open April to September: Mondays to Saturdays, 10.00 am – 6.00 pm; Sundays, 2.00 – 6.00 pm. October to March: Mondays to Saturdays, 10.00 am – 4.00 pm; Sundays, 2.00 – 4.00 pm. Admission fee charged. Tel: (01960) 365190.

DUNLUCE CASTLE
County Antrim

Like something out of a Tolkien fantasy, the ruins of Dunluce Castle have a desolate, awe-inspiring grandeur as they rise dramatically from a precipitous basaltic rock standing over a hundred-feet sheer above the wild and chill northern sea. Separated from the mainland by a deep chasm crossed only by a narrow bridge and penetrated below by a long cave, this precarious rocky outcrop occupied a position of great strategic importance that was fought over for centuries, eventually becoming, in the sixteenth century, the principal stronghold of the Mc-Donnells, "Lords of the Isles" and rulers of far-flung

Dunluce Castle

territories along the western Scottish seaboard.

Dunluce was probably used as a fort during Early Christian times and a souterrain from this period survives beneath the present ruins. Although the site is mentioned as part of the de Burgo manor of Dunseverick in the early fourteenth century, the earliest features of the castle are two large drum towers about 9 metres in diameter on the eastern side, both relics of a stronghold built here by the McQuillans after they became lords of the district (known as "the Route"), in the late fourteenth century.

Most of the castle ruins standing today were built by Sorley Boy McDonnell (1505-89) and his descendants, the first and second Earls of Antrim. The castle had been seized by Sorley Boy in 1558 after the death of his brother Colla, who had married the daughter of the McQuillan chief in 1544. Although twice evicted, first in 1565 by Shane O'Neill and again in 1584 by the Lord Deputy, Sir John Perrott, Sorley Boy managed, with the aid of artillery, to resume occupation after a short period and was officially appointed Constable of Dunluce by the Queen in 1586.

Repairs to the damage caused by the 1584 siege to the castle's landward side were probably still in progress when Sorley Boy died in 1589. New work carried out at this time included the turretted gatehouse in the Scottish manner and cannon ports in the curtain wall evidently made to accommodate cannons taken from the nearby wreck of the Spanish Armada ship the *Girona* in 1588. The north-facing Italiante *loggia* behind the south curtain probably dates to the 1560s; it is a most unusual feature but can be paralleled at a number of Scottish castles. This *loggia* was blocked by a three-storey gabled house with bay windows, a large projecting stair-well and a great hall 28 by 10 metres. It was built in 1636 for Lady Catherine, wife of Randal MacDonnell, the second earl of Antrim (1609-82), and, from an inventory dating from the period, is known to have been furnished magnificently. Lady Catherine was also possibly responsible for part of the mainland court, believed to have been built to replace the lower yard after some of its domestic ranges, including the kitchens, fell into the sea carrying with them most of the servants in 1639. After the Royalist second Earl was arrested at Dunluce in 1642 the family ceased to reside at Dunluce Castle, which gradually fell into decay, though it remained the property of the Earls of Antrim until 1928 when it was transferred to the State for preservation.

Located on the Antrim coast 2 miles W of Bushmills. NGR:
C 904414. State Care Monument. Open April to September:
Tuesdays to Fridays, 10.00 am – 7.00 pm; Saturdays,
10.00 am – 7.00 pm; Sundays, 2.00 – 4.00 pm. October to
March: Tuesdays to Fridays, 8.00 am – 4.00 pm; Saturdays,
10.00 am – 4.00 pm; Sundays, 2.00 – 4.00 pm. Admission
fee charged.

BALLYMOON CASTLE
County Carlow

Like so many Irish castles, Ballymoon has no recorded
history, but on architectural grounds it must have been
built *c.* 1290-1310. The most likely builders were the
Carew family, who evidently by this time had acquired the
district (Idrone) from the Bigods, Earls of Norfolk. The
castle – as striking as it is unusual – comprises a courtyard about 80 feet square, delimited by granite walls, 8 feet
thick and 20 feet high. No doubt these walls had alures or
wall-walks with crenellations, but these do not survive.
Some flanking protection was provided by oblong latrine
turrets projecting from three of its faces; the fourth curtain
on the west has no such defence, though the gateway on
this side, a plain arch with portcullis grooves, may originally have had a barbican in front.

Ballymoon Castle

The interior is now bare, but the walls' many embrasures, loops, fireplaces and doors bear witness to the former presence of two-storey ranges, some with cellars, that delimited the enclosure. The fine double-fireplace on the north belonged to the great hall, while such features as the cross loops with expanded terminals and "Caernarvon arches" allow us to date the castle to the turn of the thirteenth century. The castle may not have been in use for very long; indeed, some argue it was never finished.

Located 2 miles E of Bagenalstown in a field adjacent to the Fennagh road (L33). A small bridge gives access across a deep field ditch. NGR: S 738615. National Monument. Boots recommended.

CARLOW CASTLE
County Carlow

This great keep was formerly one of the most impressive Norman castles in Ireland. Only the western wall and two towers now survive, the remainder having been accidentally blown up in 1814 by "a ninny-pated physician of the name of Middleton" who leased the building for use as a lunatic asylum and "applied blasts of gunpowder for enlarging the windows and diminishing the walls, and brought down two-thirds of the pile into a rubbishy tumulus in memory of his surpassing presumption and folly".

The original keep was a three-storey rectangular block with cylindrical corner towers, probably built between 1207 and 1213 by William Marshall on the site of a motte erected by Hugh de Lacy in the 1180s. It may be the earliest example of a "four-towered" keep in the British Isles and appears to have been directly inspired by French examples, notably Nemours (Seine-et-Marne) built between 1160 and 1180. The entrance lies at first-floor level in the north wall and access to all storeys, which had timber floors, was by way of stone stairways in the thickness of the west wall.

Ownership of the castle passed to the Crown in 1306 and was later granted to the Earls of Norfolk, who held it until confiscation in 1537. It was captured by James FitzGerald in 1494, again by Silken Thomas in 1535, and changed hands a number of times before being purchased by Donough, Earl of Thomond in 1616. It fell to the Confederates in 1642 but was later returned to Thomond after being liberated by Ireton in 1650.

Located in the town centre. Access is through Corcoran's
Mineral Water factory. NGR: S 718767. National
Monument. Open weekdays only. The key can be obtained
from the factory's office.

CLOGHOUGHTER CASTLE

County Cavan

Tucked away in a remote corner of the Erne River system,
on a tiny island in Lough Oughter, stands the ruined circular tower of Cloughoughter − a modest-sized castle with
a surprisingly prominent history. It was probably begun by
William Gorm de Lacy between 1200 and 1224, possibly
on the site of a crannog, after the Normans seized parts of
the O'Rourke kingdom of Breifne. The lower two storeys
can be ascribed to this phase; it had loops but no entrance
on the ground floor, three doorways and at least two windows at first-floor level and possibly a curtain wall on the
west side.

From 1233 until the end of the seventeenth century, the
territory of East Breifne, roughly today's County Cavan,
fell under the control of the O'Reilly clan, who built up the
castle to its present height. It played an important role in
the dynastic power struggles of the O'Reillys and in con-
flicts with their former overlords, the O'Rourkes of West
Breifne, and during this time also served as a grim prison,
where some unfortunates were incarcerated for years.
When Philip O'Reilly was held here in the 1360s he had "no
allowance save a sheaf of oats for day and night and a cup
of water, so that he was compelled to drink his own urine".

After the Flight of the Earls in 1607, the castle was captured by Sir Richard Wingfield and granted to Captain
Hugh Culme, who built himself a residence on the south
shore of the lake. In the 1641 Rebellion the castle was
captured by the O'Reillys and used again as a prison; here
the old Bishop of Kilmore, William Bedell, together with
his two sons, his son-in-law and Arthur Culme, were kept
in irons in a "cold, wet and windy room almost at the top
of the tower". It was the last stronghold to fall in the
Cromwellian wars and immediately afterwards, in March
1653, was rendered useless by a massive explosion of gun
powder. During the eighteenth and nineteenth centuries the
picturesque ivy-clad ruin was depicted by a number of
artists, including William Ashford, whose fine painting of
the castle c. 1790 hung at Fota until recently. Excavation

was carried out to facilitate conservation works on the walls in 1987; most of the finds were of seventeenth-century date, including four human skeletons, three male and one female, all evidently casualties of the final fatal siege of 1653.

Located on an island in Lough Oughter 3 miles SE of Killeshandra and S of Killykeen Forest Park. NGR: H 863554. National Monument. Open access.

BUNRATTY CASTLE
County Clare

The fashion for renovating castles and using them to host "medieval banquets" may be said to have begun at Bunratty, which was restored in the 1950s under the brilliant guidance of Percy le Clerc and filled with Lord Gort's magnificent collection of medieval furniture and tapestries. It is now one of Ireland's main tourist attractions and justifiably so – for no other castle gives a more lasting impression of later medieval life.

The castle once stood on an island in a tidal creek with a view of the water-traffic entering and leaving the port of Limerick. Not surprisingly for such a strategic site, it has had quite a stirring history with a succession of castles from 1251 onwards. The present building was erected between 1450-67 by the MacNamara or MacConmara family and passed through marriage to the O'Briens c. 1500. It was remodelled by Donough O'Brien, the "Great", (fourth) Earl of Thomond, who succeeded in 1581.

Although of great size, the castle is essentially a tower house. It comprises a tall, oblong building with a square tower at each corner, linked on the north and south sides by a broad arch rising to below the top storey. The entrance door leads into a large vaulted hall above which is the magnificent great hall with its lofty timbered roof, where the Earls of Thomond held court. While there are only three storeys in the main body of the castle – with vaulted cellars below the hall – the towers have many floors and small chambers approached by a profusion of winding mural stairs. Many were bedrooms with connecting latrines, the castle having no less than fifteen privies. The fourth Earl remodelled the upper rooms of the towers; his vaulting still survives in one tower and is among the earliest use of brick in the country. Some of the Earl's plaster decoration remains in the hall, chapel and south solar and may be considered among the oldest stucco known in Ireland.

The castle's grandeur greatly impressed Archbishop Rinuccini who came here in 1646 and wrote of its great beauty, its ponds and 3,000 head of deer. But the property suffered during the seventeenth-century wars, and the O'Briens departed. It was acquired by the Studderts around 1720, who occupied a brick house built against the two northern towers and later built themselves a fine country house in the park. The castle was later used as a police barracks but subsequently fell into disrepair, and towards the end of the nineteenth century the roof of the great hall was allowed to collapse. It was acquired by Lord Gort in 1954 and since his death the castle and its contents have been held in trust for the Nation.

Located 8 miles W of Limerick on the airport road (T11). NGR: R 452610. National Monument. Open daily throughout the year: 9.30 am – 5.00 pm (last admission 4.30 pm). The Folk Park, which includes eight farmhouses, a village street, a mill and a blacksmith's forge, remains open until 7.00 pm from June to August. Admission fee charged. Tel: (061) 361511.

CARRIGAHOLT CASTLE
County Clare

Set on the verge of a cliff overlooking the Shannon Estuary, this is a tall, well-preserved tower house built around the end of the fifteenth century by the MacMahons, chiefs of the Corcabascin Peninsula. Standing in one corner of a turreted bawn, it has five storeys with a vault on the fourth floor and most of the usual tower-house features, such as a murder hole inside the entrance, a mural winding stair and pistol loops.

The castle was occupied by Teige Caech "the short-sighted" MacMahon, in September 1588 when seven ships of the Spanish Armada anchored at Carrigaholt. Although aid was refused by the MacMahons, the castle was nonetheless unsuccessfully besieged shortly afterwards by Sir Conyers Clifford. The following year the renegade fourth Earl of Thomond captured it after a four-day siege and, in breach of the surrender terms, hanged all the defenders. Ownership then passed to the Earl's brother Donal, who was responsible for inserting many of the castle's windows as well as the fireplace on the fifth floor, which bears the date 1603. Donal's grandson was the celebrated third Viscount Clare who resided at Carrigaholt and raised a regiment of horse known as the "Yellow Dragoons" for James II's armies. After the forfeiture of his extensive 57,000 acre estate by the Williamites, the castle was acquired by the Burton family who held it until the present century.

Located 7 miles SW of Kilkee on W side of the jetty at Carrigaholt. Access through field. NGR: Q 848512. National Monument.

Gleninagh Castle

GLENINAGH CASTLE
County Clare

Looking down from a hillside across the wide expanse of Galway Bay, this well-preserved sixteenth-century tower house stands guard over the northern shoreline of the Burren. It has a distinctive L-shaped plan comprising an oblong tower of four storeys with a projecting turret containing a spiral stair. The entrance doorway, which may have been moved from elsewhere, lies at first-floor level with a protecting machicolation high above in the turret. Striking round bartizans are present on three corners of the main tower, while an attic in its roof was contained behind gables on all four sides. The third storey is vaulted and there is another over a dark basement, which may have been used as a prison. In the end wall a number of window embrasures were later blocked for fireplaces.

The castle was built for the O'Loughlins (O'Lochlainns), who were still resident in the 1840s. It remained occupied until the 1890s.

Located 3 miles NW of Ballyvaughan off the coast road to Lissdoonvarna (L54). Access down a lane and across a field. NGR: M 193103. National Monument.

LEMANEAGH CASTLE
County Clare

The magnificent ruins of the great O'Brien stronghold of Lemaneagh stand on the southern fringe of that limestone wilderness known as the Burren. It is a lonely place, some call it bleak, and perhaps a surprising location for a splendid four-storey, high-gabled, early seventeenth-century mansion with rows of large mullioned and transomed windows. The early part of the building at the east end is, by contrast, a rather grim five-storey tower *c.* 1500, with narrow slit openings for windows, a tier of small chambers and a spiral stair. Its entrance passage, with drawbar holes for inner and outer doors, was probably later reserved for servants, as the gabled mansion had its own front door. Indeed, this mansion, which clearly replaced an earlier hall block on the site, is likely also to have had its own timber stair for access to the living rooms on the first and second floors, as the kitchen and offices were on the ground floor.

Defensive features connected to the later mansion appear to be few; there is a low-hung bartizan on one corner and a wing with wall-walk on the opposite side. However, it is no longer readily apparent that the building was once surrounded by a walled bawn with a projecting defensive parapet. This was entered through a fine round-headed gateway with heavy corbels and two coats of arms, one the quartered bearings of Conor O'Brien, 1643, and the other those of his son Sir Donat O'Brien, 1690. An inscription states that it was "built in the year 1643 by Conor O'Brien and by Mary ni Mahon, wife of the said Connor". Sadly, this gateway was moved in recent decades to Dromoland where it stands in the walled garden.

The castle was first mentioned in 1550 when it was granted to Donough O'Brien, Lord Inchiquin, who was hanged in 1582. It passed to the Dromoland O'Briens and

Lemaneagh Castle

by the 1630s had been inherited by Conor O'Brien, whose wife was the formidable Maire Rua (Maire ni Mahon), about whom there are many tales. It is said that she hung her disobedient men servants by the necks and her maids by the hair from the castle's corbels and used to accompany her husband on raids upon English settlers. When Conor was killed in a skirmish with Ludlow's army in 1651, she is said to have refused to open the gates to receive her stricken husband, declaring, "We need no dead men here", but having found that he was still alive nursed him until his death a few hours later. Ludlow later stayed in the castle for two nights, but found the November weather so foul that he retreated back to Limerick. It was probably during this time that Maire Rua obtained permission to marry one of his cornets, by the name of Cooper, thus managing to preserve intact the inheritance of her ten-year-old son, Sir Donat O'Brien, ancestor of the present Lords of Inchiquin. Sir Donat later embellished the extensive walled gardens at Lemaneagh, adding a canal and tree-lined avenues, but around 1705 abandoned the place for Dromoland where he died in 1717. The castle quickly became a ruin with its lower windows and doors blocked to prevent access. These windows have now been replaced, but one of Lemaneagh's fine fireplaces still remains in the Old Ground Hotel at Ennis.

Located 3 miles E of Kilfenora on the Carran/Ballyvaughan Road (L51). The site can only be seen over the low roadside wall, as the land-owner is presently preventing access to visitors. NGR: R 233937. National Monument.

NEWTOWN CASTLE
County Clare

Like a rocket on its launch-pad, this unusual sixteenth-century tower house takes the form of a cylinder impaled upon a pyramid. The whole base of the wall between the four boldly projecting spurs is commanded by shotholes ingeniously placed in the apex of pointed notches at the fusion of the cylinder and pyramid. One of these notches, or ghost-gables, lies over the door which is also commanded by one of four machicolations projecting from the parapet. Internally, the tower has five storeys with dome vaults over the ground and third storeys, both of which have well-preserved impressions of wickerwork matting. The hall on the fourth storey has mullioned windows with the spiral stair projecting into the room. The top floor, originally a bed chamber, has now been incorrectly restored as a gallery, presumably so that visitors can better admire the new conical oak roof.

The castle was originally built by a sept of the O'Briens and later passed into the hands of the O'Loughlins (O'Lochlainns) – self-styled "Princes of the Burren". It was still inhabited by the family at the end of the nineteenth century, but later fell into ruin. In 1993-94 the castle was restored as an exhibition centre for the adjacent Burren Art College.

Newtown Castle

Located 1.5 miles SW of Ballyvaghan to W of the Lisdoonvarna road (T69). Access up a quarter-mile tarred lane. Signposted. NGR: M 217064. Open all year: 10.00 am – 6.00 pm. Admission fee charged. Tel: Michael Greene on (065) 77200.

BALLYNACARRIGA CASTLE
County Cork

The hall or living-room of Irish tower houses sometimes doubled-up as a chapel, though rarely were the occupants so devotional as to embellish the room with religious carvings. The Hurleys of Ballynacarriga appear to have been an exception, for the top-floor window embrasures of their castle have stone carvings mostly of a religious nature. One of the windows has a representation of the Crucifixion with the Instruments of Passion nearby – the Crown of Thorns, a hammer and a heart pierced with two swords. The carvings are dated 1585 with the initials "R.M.C.C.", probably those of Randal Murlihy (Hurley) and his wife Catherine Collins. The opposite window has intricate carvings around a chess-board design with the figure of a woman with five roses, thought to be the blessed Virgin, though some believe it to represent Catherine Collins and her five children.

The three-storey tower house has spacious rooms with fine fireplaces, a good system of latrines and a wide mural staircase. Despite the date on the window soffit of the top floor, the castle was probably built in the mid-sixteenth century or earlier. There is a good *sheela-na-gig* above the main door, while the remnants of a round corner tower of the bawn can be seen outside the entrance. During the Confederate War of 1641-52, the Hurleys supported their overlord, Lord Muskerry (MacCarthy More), and in consequence the castle was dismantled by Cromwellian troops and their lands forfeited. It is believed that the ruin continued to serve as a chapel until 1815.

Located 4.5 miles SW of Ballineen and 1 mile S of Manch Bridge on a minor road off the T65 to Drimoleague. NGR: W 290509. National Monument. Keys may be obtained from Marion Crowley, Castlebar, Ballynacarriga. Tel: (023) 45525.

BLARNEY CASTLE
County Cork

Blarney is celebrated the world over for a stone on the parapet that is said to endow whoever kisses it with the eternal gift of eloquence. The origin of this custom is unknown, though the word "blarney", meaning to placate with soft talk or to deceive without offending, probably derives from the stream of unfulfilled promises of Cormac MacDermot MacCarthy to the Lord President of Munster in the late sixteenth century. Having seemingly agreed to deliver his castle to the Crown, he continuously delayed doing so with soft words, which came to be known as "Blarney talk".

The massive castle, which looks even larger because of its picturesque situation on the edge of a cliff, was supposedly built in 1446 by Cormac MacCarthy "the Strong", probably on the site of a castle occupied by the Lombards, whom the MacCarthys had displaced. It has an L-shaped plan with five storeys, the lower two being under a pointed vault with walls 12 feet thick; higher up the walls get thinner and the rooms bigger. The building sequence is a little puzzling, but the slender tower containing the main stair and a tier of small rooms evidently predates the main block. The whole is crowned with high stepped battlements, projecting more than 2 feet beyond the walls and carried by long inverted pyramid corbels.

The MacCarthys held onto the castle with a few interruptions until the Williamite wars, when Donagh MacCarthy, the fourth Earl of Clancarty, supported the losing side and had his estates forfeited. It is said that before leaving he cast the family silver into the lake. The property was acquired by Sir John Jefferys, who built a Gothic-style house onto the castle with pointed windows and curvilinear pinnacled battements. This was burnt *c.* 1820, but a semicircular staircase tower still remains. Nearby the family made a megalithic garden folly and in 1874 they built a Scottish Baronial-style house overlooking the lake in the park.

Located 5 miles NW of Cork on the SW side of the village within demesne. NGR: W 614753. Open June to September: Mondays to Saturdays, 12.00 – 6.00 pm. Admission fee charged. Tel: (021) 385252.

CARRIGAPHOOCA CASTLE
County Cork

Perched on a high rock overlooking the Sullane River, the tall tower house of Carrigaphooca commands truly panoramic views of the surrounding landscape. Built by Dermot Mor MacCarthy sometime between 1436 and his death in 1451, it is a very simple building with a single room on each of its five levels. The windows are very plain in form, small and narrow, and like other early tower houses, there are no fireplaces or chimneys. A mural stair of long straight flights gives access to the lower levels, while the upper floors are approached by a spiral stair in the south-east corner. The top floor, now roofless, is supported by a pointed arch, and although the battlements are now gone, there are remains of machicolations on two of the corners.

The MacCarthys of Carrigaphooca were constantly engaged in internecine warfare. They sided with the Crown in 1602 and their stronghold was consequently attacked by Donal Cam O'Sullivan Beare. After a difficult siege, the bawn walls were eventually breached and the huge wooden door of the castle burned down. The garrison was set free and O'Sullivan Beare retrieved a chest of Spanish gold he had presented to the MacCarthys some months earlier in return for their support against the English. The castle was subsequently owned by the MacCarthys of Drishane until forfeited in 1690.

Located 3 miles W of Macroom, just S of the Killarney road (N22). NGR: W 293734. National Monument. Open access. Boggy field and slippery rocks. Sturdy boots recommended.

CHARLES FORT
County Cork

Charles Fort is the most outstanding example of a seventeenth-century star-shaped fortification to survive in Ireland. It lies on the site of a medieval castle, which had belonged to the Barry Oges until 1601, when it was occupied by a Spanish force and subsequently stormed by Mountjoy's troops. In 1668 the place was chosen by the Earl of Orrey for an earthwork fort built with outer and inner lines of ramparts allowing for two tiers of guns overlooking the water.

The construction of the present fort began in 1677 to designs of Sir William Robinson, the Surveyor-General, in co-operation with the engineer James Archer, who oversaw the work. The name was changed to Charles Fort in 1681, after a visit by the Lord Lieutenant, the Duke of Ormonde. It had five bastions, known as the Charles, the Devil, the North, the Flagstaff and the Cockpit. The first two of these faced the harbour and were the main strength of the fort;

but the others were overlooked by the high ground, which proved to be the fort's great weakness. In October 1690 it was besieged by the Williamite general, the Duke of Marlborough, who succeeded in making a breach in the wall by placing his cannon on the high ground. After twelve days' siege, the aged governor, Sir Edward Scott, and 1,000 of his men surrendered on honourable terms and marched out through the breach in the walls, followed by Lady Scott in her carriage.

From 1694 onwards the fort was largely rebuilt by the Huguenot military engineer Rudolph Corneille, following the original outline. Further work was also carried out, including the the present rusticated entrance, from 1702 to 1709 by Thomas Burgh, the Surveyor-General. A barracks for over 300 men was added in the nineteenth century. In 1922 the army handed over the fort to Irish "Irregulars", who burnt it down. In 1973 it was declared a National Monument and was subsequently renovated.

Located 1.5 miles SE of Kinsale, beyond the village of Summer Cove. NGR: W 655494. National Monument. Open mid-April to mid-September: Tuesdays to Saturdays, 9.00 am – 4.30 pm, Sundays, 11.00 am – 5.30 pm. Mid-September to mid-October: Mondays to Saturdays, 9.00 am – 5.00 pm, Sundays, 10.00 am – 5.00 pm. Last admission 45 minutes before closing. Admission fee charged. Tel: Mrs Barbara McNamara on (021) 772263. For guides during the summer season, tel: (021) 72684.

CONNA CASTLE
County Cork

Resembling some sort of medieval skyscraper, this captivating tower house rises about 85 feet from a great limestone bluff overlooking the lovely rich countryside of the Brade Valley. It was built in the 1550s by Sir Thomas Roe FitzGerald, who by right should have succeeded to the title and vast lands of his father, the fourteenth Earl of Desmond. His claim was disallowed, however, in favour of his younger half-brother, Garrett, who became the fifteenth Earl of Desmond. This latter Earl, as is well known, was goaded into a rebellion in which he lost everything, including his life, in 1583. Thomas Roe took no part in this war and died peacefully at Conna in 1595, but his claim to the earldom passed to his eldest son James, who was known as the "Sugan Earl" because his claim to the title seemed sure to fail – as indeed it did. After joining the revolt in 1599, the "Sugan Earl" was betrayed by a kinsman, captured and taken to the Tower of London, where he died. That year Conna was taken by the Lord Lieutenant, the Earl of Essex, and partly dismantled. It was later granted to Richard Boyle, Earl of Cork, who repaired the property, but in 1645 it was captured by Confederate forces under Lord Castlehaven and the men of the garrison were put to the sword. The tower's history came to a sad end in 1653 when it was destroyed by a fire in which the three daughters of the steward were burnt to death.

Considering its dramatic history, the castle survives in good condition. It has five storeys, all linked by a winding mural stair, with a vault over the "Earl's room" on the first floor. Only a few fragments of the bawn remain, with a wall and outbuilding at the north-west corner.

Located 4 miles W of Tallow on the N side of the Cork road (L188). Access through a five-bar gate at E end of village. NGR: W 931936. National Monument. Key obtainable from Garda Station at Ballynoe, 2 miles S.

COPPINGER'S COURT
County Cork

The striking silhouette of this ivy-clad ruin dominates Ballyvirine – a fertile and picturesque valley west of Rosscarbery. The stronghouse was built sometime after 1612 by Sir Walter Coppinger, a prominent Cork merchant of Danish origin, after he had dubiously acquired the land through mortgages for loans issued. Sir Walter's vigorous desire to develop and modernise his estates brought him into conflict with traditional rural ways. He is therefore remembered, probably wrongly, as an awful despot who lorded it over the district, hanging anyone who disagreed with him from a gallows on a gable end of the Court. He planned to build a model village nearby, but these and other schemes foundered with the 1641 Rebellion, when the house was ransacked and partially burnt down.

The Court was probably seen as a flagship for his modernisation process, and owes little to tower houses, being without mural stairs and chambers, garderobes or vaults. It had a symmetrical "U" plan of three storeys over a raised basement with gabled attics. The entrance front was flanked by two projecting wings to form a shallow three-sided court, while a wing at the centre back, possibly added a little later, contained a grand half-turn stair. The entrance led into a long screened lobby with the hall on the left and dining-room to the right. The kitchen was in the north-west tower. The machicolations with giant pyramidal corbels are a striking feature, but sadly many of the mullioned windows have long been sold to cutlers for sharpening. So impressive was this house that it was said to have had a window for every day of the year, a chimney for every week and a door for every month. Visitors often like to count!

Located 2 miles W of Rosscarbery in a field off the Glandore road. NGR: W 260358. Wellington boots required.

KANTURK CASTLE

County Cork

The great semi-fortified Jacobean house at Kanturk (*c*. 1610) was never carried to completion after suspicious neighbours complained to the Privy Council that it was too dangerous and powerful a place to be in the hands of a subject. The builder, Dermot MacOwen Macarthy, Lord of Dunhallow, was ordered to stop work, and in a fit of rage he had the stained glass for the windows smashed and dumped in a nearby river.

The castle shell, subsequently known as "MacDonagh's Folly", consists of an impressive rectangular centre block of three storeys over a basement, flanked on each corner by communicating towers, one of which contained the timber stair. The roof was never completed, but it is likely that gables were intended to terminate the towers above a continuous machicolated parapet. There are large mullioned windows in the main block, while the main doorway has pilasters with a bold frieze and cornice – a rather barbarous but not unattractive example of provincial classicalism.

Located 12 miles W of Mallow and 1 mile S of the village in Castle Park (Poal) Demesne. Access over a stile. NGR: W 382018. National Monument.

MALLOW CASTLE
County Cork

The old Desmond fortress on the Blackwater River at Mallow was granted in 1584 to Sir Thomas Norreys, Lord President of Munster and son of Queen Elizabeth's life-long friend, Lord Norreys of Rycote. He built a "goodly strong and sumptuous house, upon the ruins of the old castle, with a bawn to it about 120 foot square" sometime between 1593 and 1599. This building, whose shell still stands, is a three-storey gabled oblong, one room thick, with an attic floor and a cellar below the centre. At the front there are two octagonal corner turrets, one for a stair and a projecting turret in the middle for the entrance. There is also a turret at the centre rear for the main stair and latrines. The style is essentially English and early Jacobean with its high gables, single-stepped battlements and large mullioned windows, but the place was well-adapted for Irish conditions with numerous loop-holes for muskets, notably in the turrets and beneath the upper windows.

Mallow Castle held out against the Confederates under Lord Mountgarret in 1642, by which time it belonged to General William Jephson, whose mother, Elizabeth – a god-child of the Queen after whom she was named – was the daughter and heiress of Sir Thomas Norreys. It was severely damaged after being captured by Lord Castlehaven in 1645 and appears to have been abandoned sometime afterwards. The Jephsons built a pleasant new house from the old stables and remained there until the 1980s.

Located on the east side of the town up from the demesne avenue. NGR: W 562983. National Monument.

CASTLEDOE
County Donegal

On a remote rocky promontory, by the upper reaches of Sheephaven Bay, stands the grim four-storey tower house and bawn of Castledoe – one of the most fought-over and disputed castles in Ireland. It was built in the 1520s by MacSweeney Doe, head of a fiery and quarrelsome tributary sept of the O'Donnells, who were constantly engaged in internecine wars usually over possession of the castle, which was besieged and captured at least twenty times before being abandoned at the close of the seventeenth century.

The halcyon years at Castledoe came during the chieftancy of Eoghan Og II MacSweeny, the foster-father of Red Hugh O'Donnell, who was famed for his hospitality, patronage of the bards and for harbouring shipwrecked sailors of the Spanish Armada. In 1596 the castle passed to his nephew, Mulmurry (later Sir Miles) MacSweeney Doe, an unsavoury tyrant who tried disobedient vassals in the castle's great hall; those of the condemned he wished to honour he brained with his club, while the less fortunate were strung up on meat hooks from the castle's parapets. It is said that in order to prevent the marriage of his daughter Eileen to Turlough Oge O'Boyle, the unfortunate man was cast into the dungeon on the third floor of the castle and starved to death.

In 1601 Red Hugh O'Donnell ousted Sir Miles from the castle, and over the next decade the place was taken and retaken by the MacSweeneys, the O'Donnells and the Crown forces. It was acquired by Captain Sandford in 1614 and described in 1623 as "an ancient strong castle, three storeys high, and a bawn of lime and stone with good flankers . . . well repaired by Sandford who hath made in it some additions of buildings and hath covered the house and slated it and is now building a house within the bawn".

The castle fell to the Confederates in 1641 and for nine years was held by Captain Donnell MacSweeney, grandson of Eoghan Og II. In July 1642 Sir Phelim O'Neill, and many of the northern leaders, greeted Owen Roe O'Neill and a hundred Irish followers at Castledoe after they arrived aboard a Spanish thirty-gun man-o'-war. The Parliamentarians captured the castle in 1650 and installed a military garrison, but in the Williamite wars it was taken by Donagh Og MacSweeney, only to be dispossessed soon afterwards.

The castle was in ruins by the 1790s when it was acquired and made habitable by General Vaughan Harte, whose arms appear over the doorway. Both the general and his son carried out extensive repairs and extensions to the castle, many of which are difficult to distinguish from the earlier features. The Hartes moved out in 1843 and in 1864 sold Castledoe in the Land Estates Courts. It was occupied by tenants until the end of the century, but afterwards allowed to fall into ruin again.

Located 2 miles NE of Creeslough on the coast. Access 300 yards down a lane. NGR: C 085318. National Monument. Open throughout the year. Admission fee charged. Tel: Gideon Moore, caretaker, on (074) 38124.

DONEGAL CASTLE
County Donegal

The site of Donegal Castle at the mouth of the River Eske was chief seat to the great clan O'Donnell, rulers of Tirconnell from the Middle Ages. Their great house — a tower house and bawn built in the sixteenth century on a rocky outcrop above the river — was later granted to Sir Basil Brooke, who remodelled it and added a fine Jacobean manor house wing soon after 1623.

The original O'Donnell tower house is believed to have been built in 1474, but existing detail suggests a mid-sixteenth-century date, while the Annals mention a "new tower" and an "old castle" at Donegal in 1564. Two years later the castle was visited by the Lord Deputy, Sir Henry Sidney, who described it as "one of the greatest that I ever saw in Ireland in any Irishman's lands and would appear in good keeping one of the fairest". It was burnt in 1589, partly demolished in 1595 and later during Brooke's occupation was overlaid with Jacobean rebuilding — so it is difficult now to explore what so impressed the Lord Deputy. Surviving early features include the spiral stair in the south angle and the whole of the ground floor, which is vaulted with corbel brackets and beam holes to support a loft floor. The entrance lay in the south end, but around 1630 this was blocked by a canted bay window added to the hall above. The chamfered door with Tudor-arched head leading into the hall also belongs to the sixteenth century; the good detailing on the chamfer reveals is worthy of note, as are the spandrels filled with a shallowly sculptured foliage pattern.

Four years after the "Flight of the Earls" in 1607, the O'Donnell lands in Donegal were granted to Captain (later Sir) Basil Brooke, a servitor of the Ulster Plantation. This grant was made permanent in 1623 and it is probable that most, if not all, the Jacobean remodelling of the O'Donnell castle took place after this date. This included rebuilding the bawn walls and flankers and the upper floors of the tower, with its two-, three- and four-mullioned windows, multigabled roof and ugly corner bartizans. The great hall on the first floor has a vast and elaborately carved fireplace, whose overmantel rises the full height of the room and is divided by paired inverted consoles framing panels carved with the armorial escutcheons of Sir Basil and his wife, Anne Leycester. The five-bay, three-storey manor house range, built with gables and mullioned windows in the English style, was probably added to the tower by Sir Basil's son, Sir Henry, after he inherited in 1633. In the 1641 Rebellion Sir Henry managed to hold the castle, though it was captured by Clanrickarde for a few days in 1651. During the Williamite wars the castle was successfully defended against the Jacobite forces. It subsequently fell into decay during the eighteenth century.

Located near the Diamond in the centre of Donegal town. At present this castle is undergoing an extensive restoration programme by the Office of Public Works and will remain shut to the public for the 1995 season.

GREENCASTLE (NORTHBURGH)
County Donegal

At first glance the shattered remains of this castle, with angular towers outlined by bands of different coloured stone, resemble the magnificent Edwardian fortress at Caernarfron. Indeed, it may have been designed by the same person, though Greencastle – called Northburgh by the Normans – was not a royal castle but was built by the "Red" Earl of Ulster, Richard de Burgo, in 1305 to help subdue the O'Neills and O'Donnells and control the entry into Lough Foyle.

The castle encompasses a lofty rock platform, whose cliffs afforded good protection on the seaward side. Like Caernarfron, it has an oblong plan with the gatehouse at one end and a large polygonal tower dominating the northeast corner. The three-storey gatehouse, which projects from the side of the rock platform, is the most impressive part of the castle and contained the main apartments. It has twin polygonal gate-towers flanking a vaulted entrance passage that gives access to the ground-floor chambers and leads up to a small sunken court and service rooms. The layout of the main chambers on the first floor resembles the gatehouse at Harlech (begun 1283), where the towers contained a private chamber with a chapel between them, while the rooms to the rear had an entrance lobby and a great chamber, the latter at Greencastle being distinguished by a large fireplace and access to a double latrine.

Once completed, the castle quickly became an important port of supply for the English armies in Scotland. Consequently, in 1316 Edward Bruce lost no time in capturing it after he had invaded Ireland. Two years later, with the death of Bruce, it reverted back to the Red Earl and later passed to his grandson, William, who was murdered near Belfast in 1333 – an event that brought about the end of de Burgo power in Ireland. The murder was an act of revenge for the death of his cousin, Walter Burke, whom William had imprisoned at Northburgh the previous year and left to starve to death. It is said that William's sister, moved by Walter's fate, endeavoured to bring him food but was detected and thrown over the battlements to the rocky shore beneath.

With the collapse of the Earldom of Ulster, the Lordship of Inishowen passed to the O'Donnells, whose dependents, the O'Dohertys, established themselves at Greencastle. The tower house on the north wall of the upper ward can be attributed to the O'Doherty occupation and was probably built in the fifteenth century. In 1555 the castle was greatly damaged during the internecine war among the O'Donnells and although later repaired and garrisoned by the O'Dohertys, it was described in 1600 as "all ruined and not much material to be rebuilt though it might annoy the ships that come by it". In 1608 the castle was granted with the rest of Inishowen to Sir Arthur Chichester, the Lord Deputy, who maintained a small garrison here until the mid-seventeenth century, when it was completely abandoned to the ivy, jackdaws and turf-scented salty air.

Located on the Inishowen shore of Lough Foyle and just E of Greencastle village. Access across a field beside Castle Inn. NGR: C 653403. Privately owned. Open public access.

AUDLEY'S CASTLE
County Down

From its rocky vantage-point overlooking the narrow entrance of Strangford Lough, this tower house is a striking landmark whose natural advantages no doubt played a key role in its siting. Built in the fifteenth century by the Audleys, one of the families introduced into Lecale by De Courcy in 1177, it is a three-storey building of the Kilclief-type with two projecting turrets containing the stair and latrines serving the upper floors. Joining them at roof level is a machicolated arch defending the entrance, set in the side wall of the stair turret. Internal features include a murder hole in the stair, fireplaces, window seats, cupboard niches and drain holes for slops, while unusually there is a stone vault roofing on the first floor rather than the ground floor.

The decline of the Audleys during the seventeenth century was mirrored by the rise of their neighbours the

Wards, who eventually purchased the property in 1765 from the descendants of the Audleys on the female line, some of whom afterwards continued to reside in Audleystown village. During the 1850s, however, the inhabitants of this settlement were shipped to America by the Wards and the area was incorporated into the landscape park.

Located on N side of Castle Ward Demesne at the end of Audleystown road. Signposted from the Downpatrick (A25) road. NGR: J 578506. State Care Monument. Open during daylight hours.

DUNDRUM CASTLE
County Down

One of Ulster's most evocative medieval ruins, Dundrum Castle was founded by the legendary Norman adventurer John de Courcy following his invasion of Ulster in 1177. The site occupies the summit of a rocky hill commanding fine views over Dundrum Bay and the plains of Lecale, controlling access into east Down from the south. De Courcy's original castle may have had defences of earth and timber, but it is probable that the stone curtain wall of the upper ward was built as early as the 1180s. As with other early *enceinte* (enclosure) walls, there were no towers, but defence was evidently aided by covered walks with machicolations along the outside wall-head. An early timber hall may have been sited near the keep, where there is a double-latrine in the curtain wall.

In 1204 de Courcy was expelled from Ulster by Hugh de Lacy who proceeded to strengthen the castle by building the massive round keep, probably employing master masons from the Welsh Marches, where such keeps were then popular. Although much of the second floor of this keep was largely rebuilt in the fifteenth century, it is clear from the survival of the old fireplace flue and spiral stair that it originally stood at least three storeys high. The basement was used for storage and had a cistern below; the first, or entrance, floor, with its large fireplace and handsome windows, appears to have been the great chamber for the lord's day-to-day living, while the floor above would have housed his private chamber.

The castle was captured by King John in 1210 and remained Crown property until de Lacy was allowed to return to his Earldom in 1226. It was probably during de Lacy's second tenure as Earl of Ulster (1227-43) that the

The castle was captured by King John in 1210 and remained Crown property until de Lacy was allowed to return to his Earldom in 1226. It was probably during de Lacy's second tenure as Earl of Ulster (1227-43) that the twin-towered gatehouse, similar to the one at Pembroke Castle, was inserted into the curtain wall. It has a lopsided design with only one projecting tower to protect the approach along a narrow ramp from the south-west.

The stone curtain wall of the outer bailey is likely to have been built by the Maginnis family, who seized Dundrum in the late fourteenth century and held it intermittently until finally expelled by Lord Mountjoy in 1601. It was made over to Lord Cromwell in 1605 and sold to Sir Francis Blundell in 1636. The Maginnis family retrieved Dundrum in 1642, but later lost it to the Parliamentarians, who dismantled the castle in 1652 after

Dundrum Castle

they withdrew their garrison. After 1660 the Blundells returned and built a gabled L-shaped mansion in the south-west corner of the outer bailey. This dwelling was ruined by the time the property passed to the second Marquess of Downshire in the early nineteenth century, though the trees on the hill were probably planted at this time. The castle and grounds were placed in State Care by the seventh Marquess in 1954.

Located just above Dundrum village. NGR: J 404370. State Care Monument. Open April to September: Tuesdays to Saturdays, 10.00 am – 7.00 pm; Sundays, 2.00 – 7.00 pm; other times by request. Small admission fee charged. Tel: (01232) 235000 extn 234.

JORDAN'S CASTLE
County Down

Ardglass was an important seaport in post-medieval times, whose defence depended upon a ring of fortified merchant's houses. The largest of these is Jordan's Castle, a four-storey tower house of fifteenth-century date, overlooking the harbour. It is the most developed example of the Kilclief-type with a stair turret and a latrine turret projecting from the north side with a high machicolation arch between them and a smaller machicolation at right angles above the entrance. The ground floor has a barrel vault with wicker-work centering marks on its soffit. The wooden floors in the upper storeys are recent reconstructions, while the present flat roof is also modern – originally the roof was probably gabled.

Little is known of the castle's history except that it withstood a lengthy siege during the Tyrone Rebellion, when Simon Jordan defended his castle for three years until relieved by the deputy Mountjoy in 1601. It probaby remained a dwelling until the late seventeenth century, but was a ruin when purchased by the antiquarian F. J. Bigger in 1911, who restored it, fitted it out with furniture and bequeathed it to the State in 1926.

Located close to Ardglass Harbour near the junction of Kildare and Quay streets. NGR: J 560372. State Care Monument. Open July and August: Tuesdays to Saturdays, 10.00 am – 7.00 pm; Sundays, 2.00 – 7.00 pm; other times by request. Small admission fee charged. Tel: (01232) 235000 extn 234.

GREENCASTLE
County Down

A popular mid-nineteenth-century travel handbook exclaimed of Greencastle, "You would go into ecstacies if you saw such ruins on the Rhine, and quote 'Childe Harold' by the canto". The fortress is impressive, though its dramatic setting at the mouth of Carlingford Lough adds much to its appeal, with views over a sweeping landscape and towering mountains beyond.

The castle was built by Hugh de Lacy almost certainly during the 1230s to protect the southern approaches to the Earldom of Ulster. It was escheated to the Crown after 1243, wrecked by the Irish in 1260 and from 1280 to 1326 was a favoured residence of the most powerful man in Ireland, Richard de Burgh, the "Red Earl" of Ulster. His daughters were raised here, including Elizabeth, who married Robert Bruce, King of Scotland, in 1302 – although this did not dissuade Edward Bruce from sacking it in 1316. After an unsuccessful siege in 1333-34, the Irish

Greencastle

captured and destroyed the castle in 1343 and 1375. The royal garrison was reduced in number *c*. 1400 as an economy measure and amalgamated with Carlingford under one constable. In 1505 it was granted to the Earls of Kildare, but after their downfall in 1534 quickly deteriorated into a "wretched condition". The place was later granted to the Bagnals who lived here until 1635. It was bombarded and destroyed by Parliamentary forces in 1652.

The design of Hugh de Lacy's castle consisted of a quadrilateral curtain wall with a D-shaped tower at each corner – all now in a very fragmentary state. Excavation of the north-east tower revealed that it had a residential use, perhaps as de Lacy's private chambers, while the rather complex south-west tower seems to have had a series of non-interconnecting rooms, suggesting its use as the private chambers of the de Lacy household. A massive surrounding rock-cut ditch was also revealed by excavation; this served as a quarry for the walls, and judging by the presence of a dam in the east ditch, may have been intended as a wet moat, though if so, the builders would have been disappointed for the rock is porous.

The castle's main feature is a large rectangular block, originally a great hall, raised upon a basement. This was lit by windows on three sides and probably had a dais at the east end for the high table, as indicated by the presence here of a high window, a small latrine and a fireplace. At the west end there was evidently a screen passage with two opposed doors, one giving access to the hall and the other the kitchens to the north. Steps led down to the dark basement store, which was later given crosswalls, vaults, gunloops and a new entrance. Remodelling of the hall in the late fifteenth and mid sixteenth centuries gave it much of its present keep-like appearance; the walls were raised at the east and west ends, turrets added at the angles, and a spiral stair, mural passages and wall-walks included.

For centuries the green below the castle played host to a great fair every August. It was often called "Ram Fair" as a great ram was customarily enthroned on top of the castle's walls.

Located 4 miles SW of Kilkeel, approached via a minor road off the A2. NGR: J 247119. State Care Monument. Open April to September: Tuesdays to Saturdays, 10.00 am – 7.00 pm; Sundays, 2.00 – 7.00 pm; other times by request. Small admission fee charged. Tel: (01232) 235000 extn 234.

KILCLIEF CASTLE
County Down

The tower house at Kilclief was built sometime between 1412 and 1433 as the summer residence of John Sely, the last Bishop and Abbot of Down (1412-41). Few tower houses can be dated so precisely, but Bishop Sely gained much notoriety for openly living in "castro de Kylcleth" with a married woman called Letys Thomb. Although the Primate served him with a monition in 1434, threatening suspension and excommunication, the Bishop obstinately persisted and was expelled from his offices in 1441. The castle was later garrisoned by the Crown and more recently was used as a farm granary.

The building stands four storeys high with projecting square turrets from its east face joined by a high machicolated arch. One of these turrets contains a latrine stack and the other a spiral stair rising to roof level. The ground-floor chamber has a barrel vault with traces of wicker centering, and the second floor has a blocked fireplace with a re-used thirteenth-century coffin-lid serving as a lintel.

Located 2.5 miles S of Strangford on the Ardglass Road. NGR: J 597457. State Care Monument. Open April to September: Tuesdays to Saturdays, 10.00am – 7.00 pm; Sundays, 2.00 – 7.00 pm; other times by request. Small admission fee charged. Tel: (01232) 235000 extn 234.

NARROW WATER CASTLE
County Down

Situated on a strategically important site where the Newry River narrows, this tower house was built by the Government around 1568 at a cost of £361. The Maginnis family of Iveagh acquired the place by 1580 and held it until the 1650s when it was forfeited. The castle was bought by the Halls in 1670, but by 1707 they were completing a new house called Mount Hall on higher ground to the north – now the staff wing of an 1836 Tudor-Revival castle.

In 1570 the tower was described as having "two chambers and a cellar and a hall covered with straw and a stable nigh unto the said castle ... and nine cottages covered with earth within the precinct of the said castle". It has three storeys and a gabled attic floor within a wall-walk, off of which is a machicolation defending the entrance. The room above the vaulted first storey has a fireplace, deep window embrasures and mural chambers in four of its corners, one for the stair and another for a latrine with external chute. The walled bawn was extensively restored in the nineteenth century, but the modern entrance probably perpetuates the site of the original gate.

Located 5 miles SE of Newry beside Warrenpoint Road. NGR: J 128194. State Care Monument. Open July and August: Tuesdays to Saturdays, 10.00 am – 7.00 pm; Sundays, 2.00 – 7.00 pm; other times by request. Small admission fee charged. Tel: (01232) 235000 extn 234.

DRIMNAGH CASTLE
County Dublin

Founded by the Barnewalls during the thirteenth century, Drimnagh Castle passed to the Loftus family in 1606 – remaining continuously occupied until 1953. It is a picturesque and modest-sized building, and its large flooded moat has recently been repaired as part of the castle's programme of restoration, which has been undertaken by a voluntary committee since 1986.

The moat probably dates from the late thirteenth-century, but the castle is quite a hotch-potch of different periods. The gateway tower – the focal feature of the complex – belongs largely to the sixteenth century; it has an arched entrance into the inner court and three upper storeys, reached by a spiral-turret stair. The adjoining building contains the great hall, restored in 1988 with a timber minstrel's gallery, an arched sandstone fireplace and a trussed oak roof modelled on the one at Dunsoghley Castle. The stone mullioned windows are early seventeenth century, while the entrance porch and stone staircase were added a century later. The formal garden in the outer court was created in 1990 featuring plants known in Ireland during the seventeenth century.

Located half a mile W of Crumlin Children's Hospital on N side of the Long Mile Road. Bus Routes 18, 50A, 56A, 77A, 77B. NGR: O 112318. Open April to October: Wednesdays, Saturdays and Sundays, 1.00 – 5.00 pm. November to March: Sundays, 2.00 – 5.00 pm. Last tour 4.30 pm. Other visits by appointment. Admission fee charged. The castle plays host to a number of conservation workshops during the year. Tel: (01) 4502530.

DUBLIN CASTLE
County Dublin

Fragments are all that remain of the great medieval fortress that once served as a symbol of Royal authority in Ireland and the centre of administration. From 1684 to 1761 it was extensively rebuilt, though the shape of the Anglo-Norman castle roughly coincides with the rebuilding. Its construction began in 1204 when King John directed Meiler Fitz-Henry, the Justiciar, to make a castle in Dublin "with good ditches and strong walls". Meiler chose a site on a ridge at the south-east corner of the city walls that was previously occupied by Henry II's "royal palace roofed with wattles" and possibly by a Hiberno-Norse forerunner. It was completed around 1228 and remained more-or-less intact until the seventeenth century.

The castle, comprising a roughly rectangular enclosure with massive drum towers at each corner, was an outstanding example of a "keepless" castle and has been compared to contemporary French castles such as Le Coudray-Salbart. Its east and south walls rose above the natural fosse provided by the River Poddle (now underground), whose waters also fed an artificial moat on its north and west sides. Excavations revealed this moat to be largely quarried from the limestone bedrock. The main gateway was sited beneath the present-day Genealogical Office, where excavations have indicated the presence of a barbarican with a drawbridge each side. The south-east or Record Tower still boasts massive thirteenth-century work two-storeys high. The 1985-87 excavations, carried out in advance of an EEC Conference Centre, exposed the base of the Corke Tower on the north-west and this, together with part of the moat, is now on view outside the new hall. Excavations around the Bermingham Tower, rebuilt in 1775, revealed the foundations of a square tower projecting from, and contemporary with, its old base. At this time excavations beneath eighteenth-century buildings exposed the full outline of the Powder Tower at the north-east corner, together with the earthen defences of the pre-Norman town below. Part of this tower, with abutting town wall and blocked moat arch, are now on display beneath Block 10.

The castle had a comparatively uneventful history and only ever had to endure one siege, when Silken Thomas made an unsuccessful and rather disorganised attempt to capture it in 1534. For many centuries it was the official residence of the Lords Deputy and Lords Lieutenant of Ireland, the home of State councils, and sometimes Parliament and the Law Courts.

Located behind the city hall with access off Castle Street. NGR: O 154339. National Monument. Open all year: Mondays to Fridays, 10.00 am – 12.15 pm; 2.00 – 5.00 pm; weekends and public holidays, 10.00 am – 5.00 pm. Not open 24-26 December and Good Friday. Admission fee charged. State apartments may be closed for state functions. Tel: (01) 6777129.

DUNSOGHLY CASTLE
County Dublin

Dunsoghly Castle

Considering the enormous number of castles in Ireland, it is perhaps surprising that only Dunsoghly has retained its original medieval trussed roof. This has survived because the castle, built around 1450 by Sir Rowland Plunkett, Chief Justice of the King's Bench, was continuously occupied until the 1870s by descendants of the same family, despite being cramped and uncomfortable by post-medieval standards. The lofty four-storey tower of the castle has tapering corner turrets rising above the parapet. The stair occupies the north-east turret, while the others contain vaulted rooms, one of which – the topmost chamber of the south-west turret – was used as a prison and is only accessible through an opening in the vault above it. The roof, which has served as a model for restorations at Bunratty Castle and Rothe House, Kilkenny, is arch-braced with four oak principals; on each collar-beam stands a king-post supporting a purlin and cross-pieces below the ridge. The rafters are laid flat rather than on edge as in modern roofs and the framework covered with split laths.

There is a small chapel to the south bearing the year 1573 over the door, the Instruments of the Passion and the initials of John Plunkett and his wife Genet Sarsfield. On the west and south are remains of earthwork defences put up during the warfare of the 1640s.

Located 2.5 miles NW of Finglas off the Slane road (N2) between Kilshane Bridge and Pass if You Can. NGR: O 118430. National Monument. Keys can be obtained from Mrs M. Walker, 4 Newtown, Dunsoghly, St Margaret's.

SWORDS CASTLE
County Dublin

Swords Castle was built as the manorial residence of the Archbishops of Dublin around 1200 or a little later. It was never strong in the military sense, but covers a large pentagonal walled area of nearly 1.5 acres with a tower on the north, probably the Constable's residence, and an impressive gateway complex on the south. The warder may have occupied the quarters to the left of the gate, while to the right was the janitor's room with the priest's room overhead. The adjoining chapel, built in the late thirteenth century, was probably used as the Archbishop's private oratory. Other buildings, recorded for an inquisition in 1326, have now vanished, including the great hall on the east side of the enclosure.

The Archbishop abandoned Swords once a new palace was built at Tallagh in 1324 – a move no doubt encouraged by damage sustained during Bruce's campaign of 1317. The stepped battlements suggest some form of occupancy during the fifteenth century, but by 1583, when briefly occupied by Dutch Protestants, it was described as

Swords Castle

"the quite spoiled old castle". It was used as a garden in the nineteenth century and sold after the Church of Ireland was disestablished.

Located at the N end of the main street of Swords. NGR: O 182469. National Monument. Key at Savage's Shop on Dublin Road.

OLD CROM CASTLE
County Fermanagh

Romantic ensemble of ruins and sham ruins set in exquisite parkland on the shores of Lough Erne. At the core of the complex are the remains of a castle built in 1611 by a Scottish planter, Michael Balfour, which in 1629 comprised a bawn 61 feet square with walls 15 feet high, two flankers and a house of "lime and stone" 22 feet square. In 1644 it was acquired by the Crichtons, ancestors of the Earls of Erne, and later enlarged so that the dwelling occupied the whole area of the bawn. It successfully withstood two ferocious Jacobite sieges in 1689, but later succumbed to an accidental fire in 1764 and was never rebuilt.

Today the remains of the castle comprise two gables and a flanker, with the remainder surviving only as foundations. In the 1830s, when the Crichtons built a grand new residence some distance to the north, these ruins were transformed into a picturesque folly with the addition of ruined walls and towers forming a sham bawn. Impressive battlemented terraces were also built around the garden to the south, where the famous pair of 400-year-old yews stand, one male and one female, at the site of the original entrance to the plantation castle garden.

Located in Crom Demesne 4 miles W of Newtownbutler. NGR: H 363238. National Trust Property. Open daily April to September: 2.00 – 6.00 pm. Car park charge at visitor centre about a quarter of a mile E of castle.

CASTLE BALFOUR
County Fermanagh

When Captain Nicholas Pynnar visited Lisnaskea in 1619 he found "great numbers of men at work" building a 70-foot square bawn and a "castle of the same length, of which one half is built two storeys high, and is to be three storeys and a half high". No definite trace of the bawn survives, but the gaunt ruins of the castle still dominate the town. Built by the Scottish planter Sir James Balfour on the site of an important Maguire stronghold, it is a thoroughly Scottish-style T-plan house with corbelled stair-turrets, parapets, high-pitched gables and chimneys. The dressed-stone entrance bay, flanked by gun-loops in the canted sides, is, however, derived from the English tradition of domestic architecture. Just inside the entrance lay a timber stair giving access to the great hall on the first floor. On the ground floor are barrel-vaulted service rooms including a kitchen with a big fireplace and circular brick-built oven.

The castle was visited and refortified in 1652 by Ludlow, the famous commander-in-chief of Cromwell's Irish armies. It was dismantled during the troubles of 1689 but reoccupied by the Balfours until 1738, when the property passed to the Townleys. The building ceased to be inhabited after a fire in 1803 and was acquired by the Crichtons of Crom in 1821.

Located in Lisnaskea adjacent to the Church of Ireland graveyard, W of the main street. NGR: H 362337. State Care Monument. Open access.

ENNISKILLEN CASTLE
County Fermanagh

All roads in Fermanagh converge on Enniskillen, which commands a vital strategic crossing of the Erne between the Upper and Lower lakes. The first castle was built here *c.* 1415 by Hugh "the Hospitable" Maguire, whose family had, by this period, secured the whole of the Erne basin. His tower house and bawn became the principal Maguire seat in 1484, but were captured and retaken many times by the O'Donnells, the O'Neills and the English, until wrecked by Niall Garbh O'Donnell in 1602. The castle became the focus of a plantation town after 1607, when the constable, William Cole, proceeded to build "a fair house upon the foundation of the old castle with other convenient houses for store and munition" and a curtain wall "26 feet high with flankers, parapet and a walk on top of the wall". This withstood a Jacobite siege in 1690 and remained the Cole family residence until a fire in 1710, when they moved to nearby Portora Castle. The ruined castle was refurbished as a barracks during the 1790s and remained in military occupation until 1950.

The rectangular three-storey keep in the middle of the castle complex incorporates the battered base of the old Maguire tower house; the upper storeys date to Cole's time and the windows to the 1790s. This building formerly lay on the east side of a bawn, separated from the rest of the island by a deep moat and entered by a draw-bridge from the north. The bawn walls, rebuilt by Cole, were removed in the 1790s to make way for the barrack complex, except those along the west side, where barrack ranges were added to the inside face.

The bawn had two circular and two rectangular flanker towers, but only the south flanker now survives – the so-called Watergate – one of the most photographed buildings in Ulster. It has a three-storey façade with stepped Irish battlements and a pair of round conical-roofed turrets corbelled low down on the angles of the building. As tall turrets are a feature of late sixteenth-century architecture in Scotland, it has been argued that the Maguires built it in the 1580s using Scottish masons. Most authorities, however, believe the Watergate was constructed around 1616-19, though it is difficult to imagine a planter like Cole, who did not even own the castle until 1620, spending much-needed resources on such a refined architectural feature – just to make the castle look more impressive from the water.

The castle keep now appropriately houses the regimental museum of the Royal Inniskilling Fusiliers. On the east side of the complex stands the recently constructed Heritage Centre, designed by local architect Richard Pierce to echo the façade of the 1796 barracks across the yard.

Located on the SW side of the island, approached from the main street via Castle Street or Wesley Street. NGR: H 231442. State Care Monument. Open May to September: Tuesdays to Fridays, 10.00 am – 5.00 pm; Saturdays and Mondays, 2.00 – 5.00 pm. July and August: Sundays, 2.00 – 5.00 pm. October to April: Tuesdays to Fridays, 10.00 am – 5.00 pm; Mondays, 2.00 – 5.00 pm. Modest admission fee. Special exhibition programmes throughout the year. Tel: (01232) 235000 extn 234.

MONEA CASTLE

County Fermanagh

Few castle ruins so readily engage the imagination as the picturesquely sited Monea – undoubtedly the most complete and best-preserved of all the Plantation castles of Ulster. Building commenced in 1616 by the Rector of Devenish, the Reverend Malcolm Hamilton. Shortly afterwards, in 1619, it was described by Pynnar as "a strong castle of lime and stone being 54 feet long and 20 feet broad". The bawn, comprising "a wall 9 feet in height and 300 feet in circuit" was added shortly before Hamilton was promoted to become Archbishop of Cashel in 1623.

Monea Castle

Like so many of Ulster's Plantation castles, the design of Monea reflects the Scottish origin of its builder. Three storeys high with tall attics, it has a rectangular plan with a pair of massive semi-cylindrical towers on the short west end. Recalling the celebrated outlines of Claypotts (1588) near Dundee, these towers are corbelled out at attic-floor level to carry diagonally placed square caphouses with crow-stepped gable roofs. The castle's only entrance lay on the south side of the north tower and led to a spiral stair giving access to the principal rooms, which, as usual, lay on the first floor and were illuminated by large windows with seats in the embrasures. The bedrooms lay in the second floor, while the vaulted ground floor, which being lit only by splayed musket-loops must have been extremely gloomy, contained the wine cellar and kitchen. Contrary to usual Scottish practice, the roof was thatched and not slated.

The walled bawn is much ruined. It was defended by round flankers at the north end, one of which was later adapted as a dovecote. The entrance lay in the north-west corner, while along the west side survive the footings of a later building, possibly a barn.

Monea's history is less dramatic than nearby Tully. During the 1641 rebellion it was attacked by Rory Maguire, who "slew and murthered eight Protestants" here, but evidently failed to capture the castle. In 1688 it was occupied by Gustavus Hamilton, the Governor of Enniskillen, who died in 1691 having incurred enormous financial losses in the Williamite wars. His greatly impoverished wife and children continued to live at Monea, but had to sell the estate in 1704. A few decades later the castle was gutted by fire and was subsequently abandoned. In the last century "a weird woman named Bell McCabe took her residence in a vault beneath one of the towers" until she was evicted by the proprietor, who feared she "might be found dead on the wretched premises,` and that some inquiries might ensue, involving the trouble incident to a coroner's inquest".

Located 6 miles NW of Enniskillen and 1 mile E of St Molaise's Church. Approached along a beech avenue through Castletown Demesne. NGR: H 165494. State Care Monument. Open public access.

TULLY CASTLE

County Fermanagh

Ireland is full of roofless ruins, but few have had such a tragically brief history as the beautifully sited Plantation castle of Tully. Comprising a stronghouse and bawn built between 1612 and 1615 for Sir John Hume of North Berwick, it was gutted and abandoned in the 1641 rebellion. The castle had been surrendered to Rory Maguire on the evening of Christmas Eve 1641 by Lady Hume on condition of safe conduct for the local Protestant settlers who had sought refuge with her. However, the "rebels having stripped the inhabitants, except Lady Hume, of all their clothes, imprisoned them in the vaults and cellars" of the castle. The men were bound hand and foot and "thrown

Tully Castle

into the courtyard where they lay all night". The next day (Christmas Day) the Maguires massacred all sixteen men and sixty-nine women and children, sparing only the Humes. They then pillaged and burnt the castle, which has remained a ruin to this day.

The Maguires would have had difficulty investing the castle by force as it was well protected. When the Commissioners visited the place in 1622 they found it had "a bawne of stone and lime 99 feet long, 9 feet broad, 10 feet high, with 4 flankers. There is also within the bawne a strong castle 54 feet long, 19 feet broad, 3 storeys high, covered with thatch." Of this, the stronghouse survives to almost full height, while the bawn wall and its rectangular flankers are ruined except for the north-east side.

The stronghouse, of two storeys with attics, has a typically Scottish T-shaped plan with a square wing projecting from the centre of the south side containing the entrance and a former scale-and-platt timber stair. The hall and parlour lay on the first floor, while the attics above contained the bedrooms, approached by a spiral stair in a Scottish-style quarter-round turret projection. The ground floor consists of a large barrel-vaulted chamber used as the kitchen and store; it has a huge fireplace and cooking recesses, but there are no windows, so light must have been provided by the fire and hanging lanterns.

A ten-year programme of repair followed the acquisition of the castle by the Department of Environment in 1974. Excavation revealed that the bawn was divided up by cobbled paths suggesting the use of this area as a garden. In 1988 formal beds were created within these paths using plants known in Ireland during the seventeenth century.

Located on the shore of Lough Erne, 3 miles N of
Derrygonnelly at the end of a laneway off the Belleek (A46)
road. NGR: H 186599. State Care Monument. Open July
and August: Tuesdays to Saturdays, 10.00 am – 7.00 pm;
Sundays, 2.00 – 7.00 pm; other times by request.
Exhibition relating to castle and gardens housed in nearby
cottage. Admission fee charged. Tel: (01232) 235000
extn 234.

AUGHNANURE CASTLE

County Galway

The "ferocious O'Flaherties", masters of the whole territory
of west Connaught, built this fine castle in the early sixteenth century, possibly on the site of a thirteenth-century
Norman fortification. It occupies a position of some
strength close to Lough Corrib on what is virtually a rocky
island formed by the Drimmeen River, separating into two
branches and reuniting at the other side – a circumstance
that gave rise to the old phrase "Aughnanure, where the
salmon come under the castle".

A natural bridge of rock gives access to the inner bawn
and tower house on the west, while an extensive outer
bawn lies to the east and south. The well-built six-storey
tower has a gracefully battered base and two flanking bartizans at mid-height, which impart to the castle a very
picturesque appearance. It has a vault over the fourth
storey with the hall on the fifth storey, where there is a
large fireplace and wide mullioned windows. A good fireplace on the third storey indicates that this was the lord's
suite, while the second, fourth and sixth storeys formed
sleeping accommodation for the family and servants. In the
thickness of the east-end wall there is a tier of mural
chambers and a spiral stair giving access to all floors. An
unusual defensive feature are the internal loopholes on the
two walls of each landing of the stair. At the top a door
leads to the wall walk and a modern hipped roof, whose
parapets have machicolations on all four sides and command a wonderful view over Lough Corrib.

Aughnanure is unusual in having a double bawn. Its
riverside walls have survived, but the east and south-east
inner curtain-walls have gone, leaving a round flanker
isolated on the south-east side. The outer ward has a similar flanker on the south-east corner, while to the west
stands one wall of the castle's once splendid banqueting-
hall. The outer wall of this building has collapsed into an

underground tributary river (now dry as its course has been changed), but its pretensions to style are evident from the carvings on the soffits of the window embrasures depicting elaborate vine leaves and clusters of grapes in low relief.

The castle was the seat of the O'Flaherty chiefs until 1572, when it was captured by Sir Edward Fitton, President of Connaught, and delivered to a junior member of the clan who had been enticed over to the Crown. Its position at the head of the lake allowed the castle to play an important role in the Cromwellian blockade of Galway, but afterwards it was forfeited and granted to the Earl of Clanrickard. Somehow the O'Flahertys remained in residence and in 1719 regained ownership, but later the castle passed to Lord St George on the foreclosure of a mortgage. In the nineteenth century a member of the Leconfield branch of the O'Flahertys planted yew trees about the castle to perpetuate its Gaelic name – the field of the yews.

Located 2 miles SE of Oughterard on a minor road E of the main Galway road. NGR: M 1544. National Monument. Open mid-June to mid-September: 9.30 am – 6.30 pm. Admisison fee charged. Caretaker: Mrs R Walsh, Knockillaree, Oughterard; tel: (091) 82214.

ARDAMULLIVAN CASTLE

County Galway

Standing on the brow of a secluded valley and surrounded by trees, this is a well-preserved early sixteenth-century tower house of the O'Shaughnessys. It has five storeys with vaults over the ground and third storeys, the former preserving its original wickerwork centering marks. The arched soffits of the north-window embrasure on the top floor have ornamental panels of stiff, stylised vine leaves – a popular form of carved decoration at that time. The mullioned windows and first-floor fireplace are evidently later insertions.

The castle is first mentioned in 1567 on the death of Sir Roger O'Shaughnessy. He was succeeded by his brother Dermot, "the Swarthy", known as "the Queen's O'Shaughnessy" for his support of the Crown. He became very unpopular in the district and indeed among his own family after he betrayed Dr Creagh, the Roman Catholic Archbishop of Armagh, who had sought refuge in the woods on O'Shaughnessy territory. In 1579 his nephew John, popular heir to the family estates and title, fought with Dermot outside the south gate of the castle and both claimants were killed. In the last century the ruin was renovated by the proprietor, Field-Marshall Viscount Gough of nearby Lough Cutra House.

Located 5 miles S of Gort due W of the main Ennis road (T11), off a minor road. On a hillock and partly hidden by trees. Access across a field. NGR: R 443950. National Monument. Caretaker is Seamus Noone, Ardmullivan.

ATHENRY CASTLE
County Galway

The great fortress and walled town of Athenry played a vital role in the Anglo-Norman control of East Connaught. Construction of the castle can be dated to between 1235-41 and was undertaken by Meiler de Bermingham after being granted a charter by William de Burgo, the Anglo-Norman conqueror of much of Connaught. It comprises a particularly well-preserved first-floor hall standing isolated within a walled enclosure, which forms part of the town's mural defences.

The main apartment of the hall block, which has two storeys over a raised basement, is entered through a doorway of notable elaboration with delicately carved capitals reminiscent of Irish Romanesque decoration. There are similar capitals and shafts on the window embrasures, while the windows themselves have fine trefoil heads. The basement was given a row of piers and vaults during the late medieval period and the building's steeply pitched gables were added about this time. The bailey has been much restored, and there is a round tower at the south-east corner and fragments of another on the north-east. Excavations in 1989 did not resolve the problematic question of the exact location and nature of the entrance, which presumably lay in the south-west corner.

The town's walls were begun in 1312 and considerable lengths can still be seen, together with flanking towers, on the west, south and south-east sides. Not long after the completion of the walls in 1316 one of the bloodiest battles of medieval Ireland was fought outside the town between Phelim O'Connor, King of Connaught, and the Anglo-Normans. The defeat of the Irish was so decisive that the constant struggle with the O'Connors came to an end — a process that seems to have resulted in a decline in the importance and strength of the town. It fell an easy prey to

Red Hugh O'Donnell in 1596 and never recovered from the damage he inflicted.

Located at the NE corner of the old town. NGR: M 512288. National Monument. Open daily June to late September: 9.30 am – 6.30 pm. Last admission 45 minutes before closing. Admission fee charged. Audio-visual show. Tel: Mrs B Sheehan, Church Street (091) 44797.

BALLYLEE

County Galway

The poet W.B. Yeats was so enchanted with this sixteenth-century tower house beside the Cloon River that he purchased the property in 1916 and restored it. For twelve years Yeats made "Thoor Ballylee" his summer home, which he found so "full of history and romance" that he was inspired to write "The Winding Stair" and "The Tower Poems". He once said: "To leave here is to leave beauty behind", and in a letter to Olivia Shakespeare wrote: "We are in our Tower and I am writing poetry as I always do here, and as always happens, no matter how I begin, it becomes love poetry before I am finished with it", and remarked "as you see I have no news, for nothing happens in this blessed place but a stray beggar or a heron."

The castle originally belonged to one of the Burke septs, ultimately forming part of the huge estates of the Earls of Clanrickarde. It stands four-storeys high and its original windows still survive in the upper part, though Yeats and his architect Professor William A. Scott installed larger windows in the lower floors. The ground-floor chamber was described by Yeats as "the pleasantest room I have yet seen, a great wide window opening over the river and a round arched door leading to the thatched hall". He also loved the mural stair, symbolically declaring "This winding, gyring, spring treadmill of a stair is my ancestral stair; That Goldsmith and the Dean, Berkeley and Burke have travelled there."

Ballylee was abandoned and started to fall into ruin in the early 1930s. For the centenary of the poet's birth in 1965, however, the place was fully restored to appear as it was when he lived there. It now also houses an interpretative centre on his life and works. Lest it be forgotten that this was once the poet's home, there is a tablet on the wall commemorating his sojourn here:

I, the poet William Yeats,
With old mill boards and sea-green slates,
And smithy work from the Gort forge,
Restored this tower for my wife George;
And may these characters remain
When all is ruin once again.

Located 4 miles NE of Gort on a minor road to the W of
the Loughrea road (L11). NGR: N 481062. Open daily May
to September: 10.00 am – 6.00 pm. Admission fee charged.
Tel: (091) 31436/63081.

DERRYHIVENNY CASTLE
County Galway

The building of true castles came more or less to an end in
Ireland with the outbreak of war in 1641 – one of the very
last being the tower house and bawn at Derryhivenny. Its
date is known from an inscription on one of its bartizan
corbels which reads "D:O'M ME:FIERI:FECIT 1643" and
states that Donal O'Madden built the castle in 1643.

A late date is supported by the absence of vaults on all
four storeys of the tower and by its picturesque diagonally
disposed Jacobean chimney-stacks. The upper rooms have
two- and three-mullioned windows with good fireplaces,
including one fine example with a plain chamfered lintel,
curved downwards at each end and covered by a chamfered
cornice. More typically, there are mural chambers and a
stair in the end wall thickness, while the main door is of
pointed form with stones ornamented with picking.

The tower forms part of an L-shaped bawn with round
flankers at diagonally opposite corners. The bawn walls
and flankers have a profusion of gunports, while the
narrow alures on the walls were probably originally extended in width by the addition of planking. Along one side
of the enclosure opposite the tower there are fragments of
a one-storey gabled building, possibly a stable block.

Located 3.5 miles N/NE of Portumna, off a minor road
lying E of the Eyrecourt road (T31). Access up lane and
across three fields. Signposted. NGR: M 872085. National
Monument. Stout footwear necessary.

FIDDAUN CASTLE
County Galway

Fiddaun is a lofty tower house that is best-known for
having one of the best-preserved bawns in Ireland. Built
during the sixteenth century for the O'Shaughnessys, it
comprises an oblong six-storey tower with vaults over its
first and fifth floors. There are square bartizans placed very
low down at third-floor level, a peculiarly Irish feature that
was brought about by the introduction of firearms, which
changed the axis of defence from the vertical to the hori-
zontal. Internally the tower has a spiral stair and a tier of
chambers in the thickness of its east end wall, with mullioned windows and a good fireplace on the fourth floor.

The tower stands isolated within a large high-walled
rectangular bawn. This is entered through a rectangular
gatehouse in the north side and has a postern on the south.
In the middle of the north end there is a salient flanker,
possibly inspired by artillery bastions of star-shaped forts.
A larger outer bawn is not walled but possesses its own
small gate building.

Most of the O'Shaugnessy estates were forfeited in 1697
when the castle's owner, Sir William O'Shaughnessy, fled
to France. Though only fifteen in 1690, he had fought as
a captain in the Jacobite cause and later in exile pursued
a brilliant military career, becoming a Mareschal de
Camp in 1734. The castle was continuously inhabited by
O'Shaughnessys until 1727, when the widow of the last
O'Shaughnessy, Lady Helena O'Kelly, died here.

Located 5 miles SW of Gort off the Tubber road, lying on a
low-level plain between two lakes. Access up a long lane
and half a mile along a path. NGR: R 409949. National
Monument. Key obtainable from Joseph Forde, Fiddaun
House; tel: (091) 331155. Wellingtons or good walking
boots are essential.

GLINSK CASTLE
County Galway

In the decades preceeding the 1641 Rebellion, a number of
Irish landowners were building houses that tried to com-
bine the need for spacious and luxurious living with an
adequate means of positive defence. Inevitably, such houses
differed from contemporary English manors in having

fewer windows, high basements, musketry loops, bartizans and other defensive features. Nonetheless, many succeeded in projecting the air of a gentleman's residence, and few more successfully than Sir Ulick Burke's handsome strong-house at Glinsk, probably begun around the time he was raised to the baronetage in 1628.

Glinsk was gutted by fire at an early stage and survives as an exceptionally well-preserved ruin. It has a three-bay rectangular plan of three storeys over a raised basement with an attic floor in its high gabled roof. The main entrance was at first-storey level on the south front, where the centre bay has been recessed, while the service door is in the centre of the north front basement. Both the door and narrow windows of the basement have flanking gunloops, while the main floors above have finely sculptured mullioned windows. The exact plan of the interior is unknown as there were only timber divisions, but the fireplaces were in the end walls where the stacks rise with tall, elegant shafts that are undoubtedly the best examples of their kind in Ireland. The house was provided with some machicolations, but had no proper flanking defence, though there was a bawn on the south side, of which one round flanker may still be seen.

Located 4 miles SE of Ballymoe off a minor road to Creggs village. Access over a stile into a field. Signposted. NGR: M 717681. National Monument. Key may be obtained from Mr Timothy Petit in the two-storey house near the castle.

PALLAS CASTLE
County Galway

The remarkably complete and well-preserved tower house at Pallas was built by the Burkes sometime around 1500. It has four storeys and an attic, the third floor being vaulted and the thick end wall containing a tier of mural chambers and a winding stair. There are attractive mullioned windows in the fourth floor (the hall) and a number of fine fireplaces on various levels, though the oven on the ground floor is a secondary addition. The lord's suite on the first floor has corner loops; other defensive features include a machicolation over the entrance and square bartizans. The roof was still thatched in the early part of the present century, the bottom being covered with stone flags for protection.

The tower stands in one corner of a large well-preserved

bawn, which has internal steps and parapets, a two-storey gatehouse (rebuilt) and a pair of round flankers with gunports. Near the tower at the west end, there is a rectangular flanker, an eighteenth-century malt-house and the remains of a large seventeenth-century gabled house. The latter had been built by the Nugents, the transplanted Jacobite Earls of Westmeath, after they were assigned the Burkes' castle and estates by the Cromwellian regime. In the 1790s the Nugents built a grand new house close to the castle to a design of William Leeson, but this was sadly demolished after the twelfth Earl of Westmeath sold Pallas around 1935.

Located 2 miles E/SE of Duniry off the Portumna road. Access up a long avenue and into backyards. Signposted. NGR: M 757074. National Monument.

PORTUMNA CASTLE
County Galway

It is no exaggeration to describe Portumna as the most important residence to be built in Ireland until Castletown a century later. In grandeur and scale it was without equal when constructed in 1616-18 and like Castletown introduced a new sophistication to Irish architecture. The builder – not surprisingly a man of great wealth and power who moved in court circles – was Richard Burke, fourth Earl of Clanrickarde, Lord President of Connaught and descendant of a Gaelic chieftaincy of Norman origin that ruled much of Connaught for centuries. His house survived the wars of the seventeenth century, only to be gutted by fire in 1826. In recent years its great shell has been re-roofed by the State.

The building belongs to a distinctive group of spacious semi-fortified rectangular houses with flanking towers at each corner. It rises to a height of three storeys, plus attics, above a raised basement and has an attractive symmetrical fenestration of regularly placed two- and three-mullioned windows and a skyline of battlements of small curved gables with pedestals and balls. At first glance it may not appear fortified, but it was surrounded by a bawn, whose wall and flankers still survive on the north side. Other defensive features included square corner-towers with gunports and a box machicolation over the main door, which despite its Renaissance pretensions had jamb shotholes and chain-holes for a grill.

The interior is two rooms deep, the rooms being separated by a double longitudinal wall enclosing a spine corridor with an oak staircase at each end. From mid eighteenth-century plans, we know that the interior was laid out in sets of state apartments in the French taste. From detailed accounts of visitors in 1808 it is apparent that the state rooms were fabulously decorated with rich stucco ceilings and friezes, handsome panelling and magnificent furnishings.

The great house was requisitioned in 1634 by the unpopular Lord Deputy Stafford to hold the celebrated inquisitions into the titles of lands in Connaught. It was lost to Henry Cromwell from 1652 to 1660 and again forfeited by William III, but restored to the tenth Earl by Queen Anne. The family continued here in great pomp until the 1826 fire. The castle laid out a fine approach from the north, with its gothic gates leading into the two great courts in front of the house. The inner court or bawn now has a restored Jacobean-style garden, though this would originally have had cut grass and statues. The early ornamental gardens lay on the east side.

Located just S of the town on the E perimeter of a formerly magnificent demesne park. NGR: M 852040. National Monument. Admission fee charged for access into the gardens. House due to open in April 1995.

CARRIGAFOYLE CASTLE
County Kerry

Carrigafoyle has had a stormy history and, although wrecked by a series of bloody sieges, remains a remarkable castle. Cleverly located between the high- and low-water marks on the shore of the Shannon Estuary, it comprises a large tower built towards the end of the fifteenth century by the O'Connors of Kerry. The tower was protected on the landward side by two square bawns, an inner one with rounded turrets and an outer with square towers at the corners. These bawns extended into the water and enclosed a small dock, so that boats could sail right up to the castle – a rather useful if not unique feature.

The tower has five storeys rising to a height of 86 feet and is beautifully constructed of specially selected small stones laid in neat courses. Each floor has an oblong chamber with a small room and spiral stair in the wall thickness at the seaward end. There are vaults over the second and fourth floors, the steep pointed arch of the latter now exposed in section by a breach of the wall on the landward side. Above can be seen small chambers in the hanches of the vault that helped to reduce its general weight and perhaps served as secret chambers.

Among the State Papers in London there is a plan of the castle dated April 1580 together with a letter to Queen Elizabeth from Lord Justice Sir William Pelham. The previous month Pelham had besieged the castle, then held for the Earl of Desmond by an Italian engineer, Captain Julian, with fifty Irish men and sixteen Spaniards. Pelham used artillery brought by sea and within two days had battered down the bawn and the western landward side of the castle. All the surviving members of the garrison were hung and the Earl of Desmond's plate, stored in the castle, was sent to the Queen. The castle was later recovered by the O'Connors, only to be surrendered again to the Lord Deputy, Sir George Carew, in 1600. It is known to have had a garrison of forty men in 1659 to protect the south shore of the Shannon. Despite its wrecked condition the castle was occupied in the last century by a Dr Fitzmaurice and his family.

Located 2 miles N of Ballylongford in the channel between the mainland and Carrig Island. Accessible from the road across a raised path of stones liable to be submerged at very high tides. NGR: Q 988474. National Monument.

ROSS CASTLE
County Kerry

There are few castles anywhere in Ireland that can boast such a dream-like enchanted setting as this ruined tower house on the shore of Killarney's Lower Lake. Built in the late fifteenth century, it is fairly typical of its type, with square bartizans on diagonally opposite corners and a thick end wall containing a tier of chambers and a winding mural stair. The tower stands within a square bawn defended by round corner towers, two of which survive, the others having been removed in 1688 to make room for an extension, the ruins of which remain on the south side of the castle.

The castle was the chief seat of the O'Donaghue Mors, hereditary rulers of this district and descendants of the ancient kings of Munster. After the Desmond rebellion, their fortified lands were acquired by the MacCarthy Mors from whom they were purchased by Sir Valentine Browne, ancestor of the Earls of Kenmare. In 1652 the castle was held by Lord Muskerry against a Cromwellian force of 1,500 foot and 700 horse soldiers, commanded by Edmond Ludlow. It fell after floating batteries were brought overland to bombard it from the lough as well as from the land. The Brownes, who retained the old faith, remained in the castle until they lost their estates in 1690 for supporting the Jacobite cause. Although their lands were recovered around 1720, they were unable to regain possession of the castle, which had been taken over as a military barracks. They subsequently built a grand new house a little further to the north, close to the town, and in time the old castle was incorporated as a picturesque feature of its landscape park.

Located 1.5 miles SW of Killarney on Ross Island within Kenmare Demesne, now incorporated within Killarney National Park. NGR: V 949887. National Monument. Open daily in May: 9.00 am – 6.00 pm; June to August: 9.00 am – 6.30 pm; September: 9.00 am – 6.00 pm; October: 9.00 am – 5.00 pm. Last admission 45 minutes before closing. Admission fee charged. Access by guided tour only. Tours limited to 15 people only. Exhibitions and excellent collection of old furniture. Tel: Henry Clifton, Killarney (064) 35851.

MAYNOOTH CASTLE
County Kildare

The tides of war have left their mark on the great castle of Maynooth – the chief residence of the all-powerful Earls of Kildare from the early fourteenth until the sixteenth century. Most of the curtain walls have now vanished, but the entrance gate and hall-keep still testify to the castle's former glory.

The massive keep, one of the largest of its kind in Ireland, probably occupies the site of an earlier castle built soon after the conquest by Gerald FitzMaurice, one of Strongbow's associates. Begun sometime around 1210, this nearly square keep was designed for two storeys, with the entrance at first floor level. Each floor was divided into two rooms, the upper level containing the lord's presence chamber and his private living-room. The building was much altered in 1426 by the sixth Earl of Kildare, who probably added the existing arched crosswall, vaults and an attic floor. The keep stood isolated within the west side of a large ward; what remains now are its eastern walls and towers, together with the main entrance gate on the south – the present entry to the castle.

In one of the first recorded uses of siege guns in Ireland, Sir William Skeffington, Henry VIII's Lord Deputy in Ireland, took Maynooth Castle in March 1535 after a week's bombardment. In the "Pardon of Maynooth" – a byword in contemporary Ireland – he put the garrison to the sword despite their having surrendered unconditionally. It was restored to the eleventh Earl of Kildare in 1552, repaired in 1630, taken by the Confederates in 1641 and dismantled at the end of the war.

Located at W end of main street to the right of gate into the college. NGR: N 938377. National Monument. Key obtainable from Mrs Saults, 9 Parson Street.

BURNCHURCH CASTLE
County Kilkenny

Many tower houses have an abundance of mural chambers and passages hidden away within their walls, though few have the number and complexity of those found in the early sixteenth-century castle of the Burncourt FitzGeralds, barons of the county Palatine. This well-preserved tower house, occupied until 1817, has four storeys beneath a vault with the principal chamber above, lying just below a gabled roof. Apart from its mullioned windows, this chamber is noteworthy for its finely carved chimney-piece, whose projecting flat arch is spanned with joggled *voussoirs* and skewbacks bearing against elbow-like stones at each end. It has a tall, round chimney, while the roof's gable walls have been extended so that both ends of the tower are carried up an extra stage to provide high battlemented fighting platforms.

A great hall was formerly attached to the tower's outside wall, but this has now vanished, as has most of the bawn – save only for a round flanker in the north-west corner. A curved outside staircase still provides access to the three upper floors of this little tower.

Located 4 miles SW of Kilkenny off the Clonmel Road (T6) at Burnchurch. Access through gate and along trackway in denuded parkland. NGR: N 472474. National Monument.

CLARA CASTLE

County Kilkenny

Anyone with a serious interest in Irish tower houses is sure to be familiar with this well-preserved example, which still retains many of its original oak doors and floor beams. Its survival owes much to having been continuously occupied from the early sixteenth century, when built by the Shortall family, until the early part of the present century.

The building has four storeys below a vault with a hall and roof attic above. Preceeded by a small seventeenth-century forecourt with musketry loopholes, the entrance leads into a small lobby with a murder hole above. On the left a winding stair occupies the north-east angle of the tower, while to the right is a small vault, perhaps used by the door-keeper. Facing the entrance another door leads into a dimly lit square room, doubtless used as a store. The oak beams of the three floors above remain in position and are about one-foot deep and wide, spaced one-foot apart, and rest on wall plates carried by stone corbels.

On the second floor, in what must have been the lord's chamber, there is a fine hooded chimney-piece, as well as a mural passage, latrine and a small room to the north, probably a bedroom. More sleeping room was available in the floor above, lying just beneath the vault, where there is also a remarkable secret chamber or strong box only reached through an opening masquerading as a lavatory seat off the top floor chamber. This latter chamber, the largest and best-lit room in the castle, was used for general family living. Its large lintelled fireplace is a secondary insertion, blocking up a window at the back, so the fireplace in this room must originally have been in the centre of the floor. The small window beside the fireplace has a sink or slop-stone below, suggesting that dishes were washed and perhaps food was cooked up here. The roof above is a modern erection, while the parapets, which are crenallated in the Irish fashion, are pierced by a large number of pistol- or musket-loops.

Located 6 miles NE of Kilkenny on a minor road 2 miles off the main Carlow road (T51). NGR: N 573579. National Monument. Key obtainable from nearby house. Wellingtons needed to cross yard.

GRANAGH CASTLE
County Kilkenny

Founded by the Le Poer family in the late thirteenth century, the castle stands dramatically on the north bank of the River Suir just above Waterford. After the attainder and execution for treason of Eustace FitzArnold Le Poer, the castle was granted in 1375 to James, second Earl of Ormonde, whose family retained possession until 1650, when it was captured by the Cromwellian regicide, Colonel Axtel, and subsequently dismantled.

The Le Poer castle comprised a large, square, walled enclosure with cylindrical corner towers. The landward side was later rebuilt by the Butlers of Ormonde, but the old river façade survives complete with its south-west tower, parts of the north-east tower, the connecting curtain wall and latrines. An adjacent walled enclosure to the south west (the outer ward) has now largely disappeared, save for a riverside drum tower. In the late fourteenth century the Butlers built a tall tower house in the north corner of the old castle and this was truncated later in the fifteenth century by a two-storey hall block built against it. The latter has vestiges of beautifully sculpted ornamentation, including an angel holding the Butler arms which decorates the inside arch of the window from which Margaret, the great Countess of Ormonde, hung rebels. The fine little oriel window in the tower was inserted during the seventeenth century.

Located 2 miles NW of Waterford on the Carrick-on-Suir Road (N24). Access over a stile. NGR: S 171145. National Monument.

KILKENNY CASTLE
County Kilkenny

Superbly set above a crossing of the River Nore, this great Norman castle has undergone many alterations over the centuries. Strongbow built a castle here as early as 1172, but this structure was destroyed by Donald O'Brien, King of Thomond. It was rebuilt in stone between 1204 and 1213 by Strongbow's son-in-law and successor, William Marshall, Earl of Pembroke. The shape of his superb "keepless" castle − built to a trapezoidal plan with massive drum towers − has been largely preserved despite the many subsequent reconstructions. Excavations in 1991-92 revealed that the original foundations on the north-west and south-west sides truncated the bank enclosing the bailey of the pre-stone castle – indicating that Strongbow's fort determined the basic outline of Marshall's fortress.

After the death of Earl Marshall, the castle was assigned to his eldest daughter, Isabel, and passed through her to the Despencers, who did not reside in Ireland. Parliament often met in the castle during the fourteenth century, which in 1307 comprised "a hall, four towers, a chapel, a motte, and divers other houses necessary to the castle". In 1391 it was sold to the Butlers, Earls of Ormonde, who after the Restoration of 1660 carried out a major rebuilding of the old castle, after it had been damaged in Cromwell's siege of 1650. Except for the classical-style gateway of 1703-06, the whole castle was again rebuilt during the 1820s in an uncompromisingly feudal-revival style by William Robertson for the first Marquess of Ormonde. In 1859-62 the picture gallery was remodelled and the castle given a number of Ruskinian features, notably a Gothic staircase. In 1935 the Ormondes ceased to live in the castle and presented it to the nation in 1967.

Located within the city of Kilkenny. NGR: S 509557. National Monument. Open daily, June to September: 10.00 am – 7.00 pm. April and May: 10.00 am – 5.00 pm. October to March: Tuesdays to Saturdays, 10.30 am – 12.45 pm and 2.00 – 5.00 pm; Sundays, 11.00 am – 12.45 pm and 2.00 – 5.00 pm. Guided tours available. Art gallery and restaurant in basement. Admission fee charged. Tel: (056) 21450.

DUNAMASE CASTLE
County Laois

The battered remains of this once-strong castle crowns a massive rock with superb views over the pass through the West Wicklow hills. It was built in the thirteenth century by William Marshall and his son-in-law William de Braose on the site of an Irish fort that Strongbow had obtained through his marriage to Dermot MacMurrough's daughter, Aoife. It had a number of owners, notably Roger de Mortimer – who further fortified it – before it fell into the hands of the O'Mores in the mid-fourteenth century. In 1641 it was taken from the O'Mores by Sir Charles Coote, retaken by Eoghan O'Neill in 1646 and finally captured and dismantled by the Cromwellians in 1650.

William Marshall probably began the enormous rectangular tower on top of the hill. Much of the southern part has now vanished, while the northern portion was remodelled to form a stronghouse in the sixteenth century and a tower was added to the west wall flanking the entrance. The surrounding walls of the inner bailey were probably built by William de Braose around 1250. These are strongest on the vulnerable east side where there is a gateway flanked by oblong towers containing guard-rooms. Below is a triangular outer ward of unknown date, entered from the east by a round-faced gate tower with traces of a drawbridge.

Located 3 miles W of Stradbally overlooking (to the N) the N80 road to Port Laoise (Maryborough). NGR: S 523980. National Monument.

LEA (LEGHE) CASTLE
County Laois

Cromwellian troops dismantled some of Ireland's finest castles − not least of which was the great fortress of Lea. The core of the castle is a massive four-towered keep that bears such a striking resemblance to Carlow Castle that they must be contemporary, especially as both were owned by William Marshall. It therefore belongs to the early thirteenth century and may well be the castle mentioned here in 1203; if so, it must be one of the earliest of these distinctive castles comprising a rectangular block with cylindrical corner towers. Sadly, only one tower now stands to any height, but the main block had three storeys over a basement and like Carlow has a first-floor doorway by the north-east tower and a straight stair in the north wall. It has single-loop openings, except for a window in the north side − probably a later insertion of c. 1250 by the FitzGeralds.

The keep was enclosed within an oval bailey whose walls still stand on the north-east side, complete with an entrance and two D-shaped bastions. Close to the latter is an outer twin-towered gateway with portcullis grooves, evidently built in 1297, giving access to a large outer bailey which runs down to the River Barrow. This gateway was later blocked for residential purposes and a latrine turret added to one side.

Few castles have had such an active history. Lea was

burnt in 1285 by the O'Connors, in 1307 by O'More and in 1315 by Bruce, after which the adjacent town was abandoned. The castle was subsequently captured on many occasions and passed to the O'Mores, the FitzGeralds, the Earls of Ormonde and the O'Dempseys, before Cromwellian troops finally wrecked it in 1650. In the eighteenth century the celebrated horse-thief James Dempsey used the vaults of the keep as his stables.

Located 2.5 miles E of Portarlington on a minor road N of the Monasterevin road (L108), between the canal and Barrow River. Access through farmyard and across a field. Signposted. NGR: N 571121.

PARKE'S CASTLE
County Leitrim

Rising from the tranquil waters of Lough Gill, this attractive Plantation castle has recently undergone an extensive restoration. It now appears much as it did around 1610, when Robert Parker completed his fortified manor house on the site of a fifteenth-century O'Rorke castle. The walls of the original bawn – a spacious pentagonal area – were retained, but the O'Rorke tower house in the centre was demolished and its stones used to build the three-storey manor on the eastern side. This has now had its window glazing reinstated, while local craftsmen have successfully restored the timber stair, as well as the mortice and tenon oak roof. One of two round flankers, protecting the bawn's north side, forms one end of the manor, while at the other end stands a gatebuilding with an arched entrance leading into the enclosure. There is also a postern gate and a sallyport, through there are no flankers on the lake shore, probably as the water level was 10 feet higher in the seventeenth century and lapped up against the bawn walls. No doubt these waters fed the moat that formerly surrounded the bawn.

Excavations revealed the base of the O'Rorke tower house beneath the courtyard cobbles in 1972-73, and this is now exposed to view. It was in this tower that Francisco de Cuellar, the shipwrecked Armada officer, was entertained by Brian O'Rorke. In later years de Cuellar was to write of his host: "Although this chief is a savage, he is a good Christian and an enemy of the heretics and is always at war with them". He was eventually captured, indicted and executed for high treason in London in 1591. The Parkers,

Parke's Castle

who subsequently acquired his confiscated property, remained at Newtown, or Leitrim Castle – as it was formerly known – until the end of the seventeenth century, when it was deserted.

Located 4 miles NW of Dromahaire on the Sligo road (R286) beside Lough Gill. NGR: G 783354. State Care Monument. Open March 17 – 20: 10.00 am – 5.00 pm. April to June: Tuesdays to Sundays, 10.00 am – 5.00 pm. July to mid-September: Tuesdays to Sundays, 9.30 am – 6.30 pm. October: Tuesdays to Saturdays, 9.00 am – 5.00 pm, Sundays 10.00 am – 5.00 pm. Admission fee charged. Tea room, exhibitions and audio-visual shop. Tel: Con Healy, Fivemilebridge (071) 61149.

ADARE CASTLE
County Limerick

The time-worn remains of this Anglo-Norman fortress on the banks of the River Maigue may be counted among the most impressive castles in Ireland. It was first mentioned in 1226 as being held by Geoffrey de Marisco, but later passed to the FitzGeralds, possibly as early as 1240. The Earls of Kildare retained ownership for nearly 300 years – until Silken Thomas's rebellion of 1536, when it was forfeited and granted to the Earl of Desmond. Barely forty years later, in 1578, the Munster Geraldines were themselves in rebellion and lost the castle to English troops after an eleven-day siege. Attempts to retrieve the castle resulted in a series of notably bloody sieges in 1579, 1581 and 1600, leaving the fabric badly damaged. It was finally dismantled by Parliamentary troops in 1657.

The castle was probably begun in the 1190s and initially comprised a large square tower and an enclosing D-shaped fosse, together with a hall block to the south in an outer ward. The tower, notable for having corner turrets projecting from the side walls, was remodelled in the fifteenth century and is thus difficult to assess confidently, though it appears originally to have had three storeys with a first-floor entrance. No doubt it served as the lord's accommodation and thus complemented the more public function of the Great Hall by the river, which was clearly built to entertain visitors: a spacious rectangular apartment with round-headed lights with roll mouldings. At a later period its basement was subdivided and a latrine added on the south side.

The curtain walls around the inner ward and along the west side of the outer ward were possibly built around 1240, no doubt replacing timber palisades. The inner ward has a south gate tower and an open-gorged bastion on the west side, while there is a square west-gate tower into the outer ward. The very ruined aisled Great Hall, to the east of the old hall, may have been added in 1326 when the second Earl of Kildare undertook extensive works at the castle. It is flanked by kitchens and service rooms, which extend to the eastern perimeter of the outer ward – whose well-preserved battlemented walls may be largely fifteenth century in date.

Located 9 miles SW of Limerick on the E side of the main road into Adare (T11). NGR: R 471467. National Monument. The castle is in a dangerous condition, but plans are in effect for a programme of conservation. There is a new heritage centre nearby; tel: (061) 396666.

ASKEATON CASTLE
County Limerick

The splendid castle of the Munster Geraldines at Askeaton, the principal seat of the last Earls of Desmond, rises majestically above the River Deel on a small rocky island. Most of the ruins belong to the fifteenth century, though they incorporate parts of a much older fortress that was founded here by William de Burgo in 1199. The Earls of

Desmond had many changes in fortune after they acquired the place in the 1340s, but the heyday of their great wealth and power undoubtedly came when the King, otherwise engaged in French wars, surrendered his royal rights in Munster to James, the seventh Earl of Desmond. It was during this time from 1420 to 1457 that most of the castle and nearby Franciscan friary were built.

The castle extends over two courtyards – an upper ward crowning the rock and a lower ward surrounding it. The upper ward still retains fragments of its thirteenth-century polygonal wall with footings of a gateway on the east side. At the northern end stands a large fifteenth century hall and chamber block, probably on thirteenth-century foundations, with the remains of a lofty narrow tower containing small rooms, latrines and a fine fireplace on the third floor. In the outer ward, built against the ramparts on the west side, stands the celebrated banqueting hall – perhaps the finest secular building of its period in Ireland. Its foundations are early medieval, but the ground-floor vaulted chambers, cellars and kitchens all belong to the 1430s, when the seventh Earl built the hall above – a magnificent room 72 feet long and 30 feet wide. A striking feature are the large windows with decorated carvings, while the south end is decorated with a blind arcade, behind which stands the remains of a chapel block. The hall was built for state occasions and it was here that the young Florentine Giovanni de Gherardini was lavishly entertained when he came to visit his Geraldine kindred in 1440.

During the Desmond rebellion, in 1580, the castle fell to Pelham after two days' bombardment, and shortly afterwards was handed over to the Berkleys. In 1599 the Earl of Essex came to its relief after it had withstood a 147-day siege by the "Sugan" Earl of Desmond. It was captured by the Confederates in 1642 and ten years later dismantled by Cromwellian troops.

Located 16 miles W/SW of Limerick on the T68. NGR: R 341501. At present, conservation work may temporarily prevent visitor access. Keyholder: T Casey, Bridge House.

CARRIGOGUNNELL CASTLE
County Limerick

From its superb vantage point on a volcanic crag, this fortress is a striking landmark which demonstrates an excellent use of natural defences. It is mentioned in thirteenth-century contexts, but the greater part of the present remains belong to the period after 1449 when the sixth Earl of Desmond conferred it on Brien Duff O'Brien, son of the Prince of Thomond. Brien and his son Donough, who died in 1505, were evidently responsible for the large multi-sided walled enclosure and the small inner ward on the north side. It has a rather complex range of buildings, including a four-storey tower, a circular bastion and a gabled house. In 1536 the castle was surrendered to Lord Deputy Grey, after he used his artillery to blow up the gate of the outer court. The men of the garrison, who were found huddled in the dungeon, were all taken out and executed. The O'Briens later lost the castle in the Cromwellian forfeitures. In 1691 it was mined and blown up with an enormous quantity of gunpowder by order of General Ginckel, after it had surrendered with its Jacobite garrison of 150 men.

Located 2 miles NW of Mungret on a minor road and up a long, straight lane for half a mile. NGR: R 499552.

LIMERICK CASTLE
County Limerick

This striking landmark in Limerick, known as "King John's Castle", stands on the east bank of the Shannon within the city walls, commanding a strategically important river crossing. It was built as a royal fortress in the early thirteenth century and is an outstanding example of a "keepless" castle, similar in many respects to contemporary castles at Kilkenny and Dublin. It has a pentagonal plan with massive drum towers defending each of the four main angles – one of which was replaced by a diamond-shaped bastion in 1611. Near the centre of the north curtain stands the main entrance, with a pointed arch and traces of a port-cullis above, flanked by two massive D-shaped towers. A flight of steps now leads up to this entrance, but originally there was a drawbridge.

The Normans appear to have attempted to secure control of Limerick around 1202 when the Annals record a "castle there". Stone-revetted earthen banks, recently dis-covered during excavations, may be part of this early Norman fort. Work on the stone castle may have begun a little later, perhaps around 1210, as the Pipe Rolls record an expenditure of £733 on the site in 1212. The twin-towered gate-building could be slightly later and perhaps was included in a payment of £522 made in 1235. It is likely that a huge sum paid out in 1280 included work on the Great Hall, which appears to have stood close to the west curtain, overlooking the Shannon.

For most of its history the castle remained in Crown control and had an uninterrupted line of constables from 1216 until the death of Lord Gort in 1842. Despite this continuity, the castle did not escape being captured on many occasions. It fell to Bruce in 1316 and later again to the O'Briens and MacNamaras in 1369. In 1642 it was taken by a strong force of Irish, after they ignited mines and breached the walls. Recent excavations in the vicinity of the east curtain wall has uncovered a fascinating series of mines and countermines dug during this siege. The castle was captured by Cromwellian troops in 1651 and by Williamite troops in 1691.

In the eighteenth century the towers were reduced in height and fitted to bear artillery. Barrack buildings were also completed in 1751 and remained in use until 1922. These were partly replaced by Corporation houses in 1935, but in 1990 the whole interior was cleared and a new visitor centre erected. Ongoing archaeological excavation, supported by Shannon Heritage, continues in the castle every summer.

Located on the N side of town by Thomond Bridge. NGR: R 582576. Open mid-April to October: Mondays to Fridays, 9.30 am – 5.30 pm; Saturdays and Sundays, 12.00 am – 5.30 pm. November to March: Saturdays and Sundays, 12.00 am – 5.30 pm (last admission one hour before closing). Admission fee charged. Group bookings for day or night. Visitors by pre-arrangement, tel: (061) 361511.

SHANID CASTLE

County Limerick

The famous war-cry and motto of the Earls of Desmond, "Shanid aboo", echoed a belief that this little castle was "Desmond's first and most ancient house". It was built by Thomas, son of Maurice FitzGerald, after he had been granted the land by the justiciar Hamo de Valognes around 1198. The castle comprises the shattered shell of a polygonal tower spectacularly clinging to the summit of a large earthen motte with surrounding fosse and bank. The tower is circular internally and only half survives to full parapet

height. It was surrounded by a curtain wall around the
summit of the earthwork; the remains on the south side still
retain some of their battlements and loop-holes. A small
kidney-shaped bailey on the east side has no sign of an
enclosing wall. It was captured by Red Hugh O'Donnell in
1601 and wrecked in 1641.

Located 8 miles N of Newcastle West off a minor road to
Glin from the L28. Access over a fence and up a hill.
NGR: R 243452.

CARLINGFORD CASTLE
County Louth

Looking down from a rock above the medieval walled
town, this striking fortress stands guard over the harbour
and the narrow pass between the town and the lofty
mountains of the Cooley Peninsula. Historical references to
the castle are sparce, but on architectural grounds it was
most likely begun around 1200, probably by Hugh de
Lacy. King John stayed here for three days in 1210, and
later that century the eastern side of the castle was
remodelled.

The original fortification evidently consisted of a many-
sided curtain wall enclosing a roughly oval area around the
summit of the rock. This survives around the western portion of the castle's courtyard, together with a flanking
tower and the remains of a twin-towered gatehouse. The
wall had two storey ranges against its inner face and was
pierced by small loops set in wide embrasures. Only
portions of the northern gatehouse tower survive, but it
is evident the gate towers flanked a surprisingly narrow
entrance passage. The well-preserved square tower in the
curtain's south-west angle is noteworthy for the way its
plan changes to a half-octagon on the upper levels – a
feature that recalls the west gate tower at Trim.

The massive cross-wall of the castle was probably added
in 1262 when records in a pipe roll show substantial pay-
ments being made for stone, timber and lead for building
works at Carlingford. At this time, much of the eastern
section of the castle was also remodelled to create three-
storey apartments and a great hall. A four-storey range was
added to the southern portion of this block in the fifteenth
century; this is now ruined but has some interesting
fireplaces and arcading.

Carlingford appears to have remained in English hands

during the post-medieval period. In 1596 Hugh O'Neill, Earl of Tyrone, tried to take the castle in a surprise attack. It was captured by Sir Henry Tichborne (Royalist) in 1642, surrendered to Lord Inchiquin (Royalist) in 1649 and delivered up to Sir Charles Coote (Cromwellian) the following year. It is likely Coote dismantled the castle, for it plays no further role in Irish history, though the town was used as a hospital station during the Williamite wars.

Located on N side of harbour and adjacent to coast road. NGR: J 188120. National Monument. No admission charged. The keyholder is Benedict Fretwell, Castlehill. Enquiries should be made at the local heritage centre.

CASTLEROCHE
County Louth

Still known by its simple Norman-French name of Roche, this impressive castle clings dramatically to the summit of a great rocky outcrop. Striking and powerful, it commands a pass northwards and affords wonderful views over the surrounding country. According to the Close Rolls of 1236 it was raised by Lady Rohesia de Vernon, whose grandfather came to Ireland with Prince John in 1185. There is a tale that she promised herself in marriage to the architect if he completed the job to her satisfaction, but when he came to claim her hand, she had him cast from one of the windows in the west end – still popularly known as "the Murder Window".

Most of the castle was built in the 1230s, though it may have been completed in the following decade. Its peculiar triangular layout, determined by the shape of the rock, comprises a large *enceinte* enclosure with a twin-towered gatehouse on the east linked to a very considerable Great Hall to the south. The high curtain walls retain their merlons, and at the north-east angle stand the remains of a four-storey D-shaped tower with wickercentering on its ground-floor vault. Wickercentering also appears on one of the ground-floor vaults of the entrance towers, which likewise had four storeys but now only retain their semi-circular front walls. A causeway gives access to the entrance across a rock-cut ditch, in the centre of which was a gap with drawbridge protected by a barbican.

The large rectangular hall in the south-east angle of the ward must have been an impressive building in its heyday. Its main chamber, lit on the south side by three large windows, was so enormous that the basement must have had timber subdividing to support the floor. The east gabled wall survives with some traces of the old roof line and indications of a third storey. A small rectangular building on the north side of the hall is a later addition, while the remains of a free-standing rectangular structure in the ward centre may also be a later feature.

Located 4.5 miles NW of Dundalk, over a stile and across a field. Signposted. NGR: H 996132. National Monument.

ROODSTOWN CASTLE
County Louth

Tower houses became a widespread phenomenon in late medieval Ireland following the collapse of central authority and the resurgence of Gaelic lords. Roodstown is a well-preserved, though roofless, example of such a residential tower, with all the typical features – a vaulted ground-floor cellar, a murder-hole inside the main entrance, a well-defended parapet and wall-walk. It has four storeys with two angle-turrets at diagonally opposite corners, one for the winding stair and the other for the latrines. The windows on the first and second floors have nicely carved fifteenth-century cusped ogee-headed lights, all with glazing bar holes. The two largest windows, both double lights and one with a transome bar, are in the first-floor hall, which also typically has the largest fireplace. As is usual in such buildings, the third floor – probably the private chamber – was unheated and had only small rectangular windows.

Located 2.5 miles E of Ardee on the Stabannon road. NGR: N 996925. National Monument. Key obtainable from Michael MacMahon, Roodstown. Tel: (041) 53647.

ROCKFLEET CASTLE
County Mayo

Visitors to this relatively small tower house cannot fail to be delighted by the elegant simplicity of its architecture and by the stark beauty of its setting on an inlet of Crew Bay.

But the principal attraction of this romantic place is its association with the legendary Grainne ni Mhaille, Grace O'Malley, who lived here after she married Sir Richard Burke (Richard the Iron), her second husband, in 1566. Few figures in Irish history catch the imagination more than this remarkable woman, known as the "Pirate Queen", for her undisputed control over the west coast in the late sixteenth century. Her navy routed large Government seaborne expeditions sent against Rockfleet in 1574 and 1579, while in 1588 she captured ships of the dispersed Spanish Armada and mercilessly killed the crews – an exploit which resulted in her being received in great state by Queen Elizabeth. After the death of her husband in 1583 she remained at Rockfleet with "all her followers and 1,000 head of cows and mares".

The castle has four storeys with a small rectangular corner turret rising above the parapet. The principal apartment must have been in the top floor where there is a fireplace. After the last war the building was restored by the diplomat Sir Owen O'Malley, a direct descendant of Grace, who lived in the nearby late Georgian house. In more recent years it was acquired by a former American ambassador to Ireland.

Located 5 miles W of Newport off the N59. Access 1 mile down a lane. NGR: L 915954. Key from Michael Chambers, Rossyvenna, Carrowbeg.

ATHLUMNEY CASTLE
County Meath

Tower houses often provided the nucleus for the unfortified country seats that began to emerge in Ireland from the seventeenth century. Many remain occupied to the present day, but Athlumney, on the east bank of the Boyne, has long been in ruins. It comprises a mid-fifteenth-century tower house, built by the Dowdall family, which was considerably enlarged around 1630 by a long, narrow gabled mansion with large mullioned windows and a fine oriel window. The tower house has four storeys, with an attic, and four projecting corner turrets of different sizes containing the stair, latrines and small chambers. In the south wall of the first floor there is a secret mural chamber reached down narrow stairs from above – created, one assumes, to hide priests, for the Dowdalls remained strong Catholics.

The mansion was burnt in 1649 as "one of ye families

Athlumney Castle

of ye Maguires was living in it when Oliver Cromwell took
Drogheda and to prevent Oliver from getting any shelter or
subsistence there, set ye stately fabric on fire which
consumed all ye curious apartments which were said to be
very rich and costly".

Located 1 mile SE of Navan off the Duleek (L5) road.
NGR: N 887664. National Monument. Key obtainable from
the convent.

DONORE CASTLE
County Meath

The small tower house of Donore may have been built with
the premium of £10 that the Government – alarmed by the
frequent incursions of Gaelic lords – offered in 1429 to
"every liege man" in the Pale who would build "a castle or
tower sufficiently embattled or fortified within the next ten
years to wit 20 feet in length 16 feet in width and 40 feet
in height or more". The inside measurements and height of
this simple three-storey rectangular tower certainly meet
those requirements. Typically, its lower storeys are
vaulted, while it has double-splayed basement loops, a
box-machicolation above the ground-floor entrance, mural
latrine chambers, rounded external corners and a projecting tower at the south-west corner containing the stair.

Donore Castle

The little castle came to a very sad end. After it was captured in 1650, the occupants at the time – James, son of MaGeoghegan, and over forty members of his household, including women and children – were all put to death by the Cromwellian general John Reynolds.

Located 8 miles SW of Trim on the Kinnegad Road (T26), about half a mile W of Inchamore Bridge. NGR: N 702497. National Monument. Key obtainable from the cottage opposite.

TRIM CASTLE
County Meath

Trim Castle is the largest and one of the most important Norman military constructions in Ireland. Its well-deserved reputation as the king of Irish castles rests upon its imposing curtain walls enclosing over three acres, its fine gatehouses, and its enormous isolated keep – all of which project a visually striking image of foreboding might and great power.

The first fortification on this site above the banks of the Boyne was a motte erected by Hugh de Lacy in 1172. After this was destroyed by Roderick of Connaught in 1174, de

Lacy embarked on building another castle, the nature of which has not yet been established. On the basis of the present limited evidence, it seems likely that the curtain wall and the huge stone keep, which envelopes the stump of the old motte, were begun by de Lacy during the 1170s. Structural examination of the keep has shown that it was built in two major phases, which were probably close together but not continuous. It is thought that this break in construction corresponds with the minority of Hugh de Lacy's eldest son Walter between 1186 and 1194, when the Lordship was held by Prince John. Work may still have been proceeding when King John came here in 1210, for the following year, after the Crown had taken control of the castle, the sum of £64 was spent on building work, including "22/- for a large horse . . . for strengthening the tower". The keep was probably being completed around this time.

The design of the keep is most unusual, comprising a massive square block with towers projecting from the middle of each face (only three out of the original four remain). On plan it looks like a combination of a square and a Greek cross. The towers have thinner walls than the main core and appear to have been added, not for defensive reasons, but to provide extra rooms and possibly because they looked good. Three of the four projections have

Trim Castle

ground floors, but the main core of the keep at this level is evidently filled with earth. The entrance is within the east tower at first-floor level, below the chapel, and access to the three floors of the centre block is provided by a mural winding stair in the south-west and north-east angles. The first floor and second floors are divided by a central wall, but the third floor was one large apartment and was clearly the main room in the castle – most probably the lord's chamber. Mural passages gave access to the rooms in the side-towers, though on the top floor galleries linked some of these subsidiary rooms with one another, without needing to enter the centre block at all.

The curtain walls at Trim, two-thirds of which still stand, had a perimeter of 500 yards. They must have been completed by 1224 when William Marshall, the justiciar, besieged the castle for seven weeks, for it is unlikely the castle could have withstood his army for such a period without the protection of the curtain walls. The remains now consist of two sections, the first comprising the west gatehouse and the wall from it to the northern tower, while the second comprises the vulnerable southern curtain with its five D-shaped towers and circular east gatehouse. It has been argued that the rectangular west gatehouse is earlier because its vaulted passage uses round, rather than pointed, arches, but this is conjectural. There appears to have been a barbican on the town side of the west entrance, which was further protected by a murder hole, a portcullis, the gate, and a second murder hole through a hole in the passage. Barbicans only rarely survive, but the east gatehouse entrance passage is continued outwards between two crenellated walls to a fine barbican on the outer edge of the moat. It is often claimed that the upper rooms of this gatehouse were used to house the young Prince Hal, later Henry V, who was left at Trim by Richard II in 1399 before his fateful return to England.

An extensive excavation was carried out between 1971 and 1974 in the area between the keep and the south curtain wall. This revealed a stone plinth added to the keep, parts of a ditch possibly dug around the keep and a number of ancillary buildings. It is to be hoped that more excavations will be carried out in the keep itself and in the area near the north tower, where it is evident that the Great Hall of the castle once stood.

Located 28 miles NW of Dublin on the SE side of the old town. NGR: N 202564. National Monument. The keep is presently under conservation, but visitors can gain access to the bailey, either through the west gate (if open) or by walking around the walls to the Boyne front.

BALLINTOBER CASTLE

County Roscommon

This large "keepless" fortress is often claimed to be the only surviving early medieval castle of an Irish ruler. It was built in the 1290s and has a roughly square plan, with enormous asymmetrical polygonal corner towers and a gateway in the eastern curtain, flanked by comparatively small projecting turrets. However, residential apartments in the upper floors of the towers appear quite sophisticated in their design, indicating that Norman rather than Irish architects were employed. Indeed, the oft-repeated claim that this castle was built by the O'Connors of the Royal House of Connaught is difficult to sustain, especially as Irish chiefs of this period had no use for such fortresses. Furthermore, in the 1333 inquisition of the Earldom of Ulster, a hundred court is recorded at Ballintober. It is likely the builder was William de Burgo, and no doubt the castle's large area was intended to permit an Anglo-Norman settlement within its walls. The northern towers are higher than the others as they were rebuilt and repaired in 1627. Outside the walls extra protection was afforded by a wide water-filled moat.

The castle fell into the hands of the O'Connors by the mid-fourteenth-century and remained in their possession for many centuries, being the chief seat of the O'Connor Don from 1385 until 1652. In 1598 it was surrendered to Red Hugh O'Donnell, who attacked it with cannon, breached its walls and forced Hugh O'Connor Don to re-cant his allegiance to the Crown. In 1641 it became a centre of Catholic resistance with the result that it was confiscated in 1652 and assigned to the transplanted Lord Kilmallock. The O'Connors regained possession in 1677 and remained in residence until 1701, when it was abandoned.

Located 11 miles NW of Roscommon off the Tulsk road (L98). Access direct from road. NGR: M 729748.

RINNDUIN CASTLE

County Roscommon

The impressive ruins on the remote Rinnduin Peninsula at Lough Ree have quite a romantic appeal, though they are very overgrown and frustrating to study. The first castle and town was founded here by the justiciar Geoffrey de Marisco in 1227 as a base during his campaign west of the

Shannon. Once the Normans secured a greater foothold in Connaught, Rinnduin assumed an increasingly important position in government military strategy. By the 1270s it was providing a vital link between the royal forts of Roscommon and Athlone, as well as guarding the ships along the Shannon and helping to keep the O'Connor kings of Connaught in check.

The castle is protected by a wide moat, once filled with water, running across the peninsula. This was probably dug in 1227, but the ward wall behind, which has small square loopholes, may not have been completed until 1260. The ward was entered through a rounded-headed archway of cut limestone with slots for a portcullis, outside of which are masonry piers for a bridge that was repaired in 1278. Near the entrance and incorporated into the ward defences is a first-floor rectangular hall, which still survives. It was built between 1299 and 1302, but the longitudinal crosswalls and vaults of its basement are later.

A town developed under the protection of the castle, which was defended on the landward side by a substantial towered wall. Virtually all traces of this town have gone, though the ruins of the parish church remain, to the east of the castle. The town was sacked by the O'Connors in 1236 and 1270. After its final plunder in 1315 it appears not to have recovered.

Located 11 miles N of Athlone and 2.5 miles E of Lecarrow. Access through fields for half a mile to end of peninsula. NGR: N 008539.

ROSCOMMON CASTLE
County Roscommon

Strategically set deep in the plains of Connaught, this great royal fortress was raised as part of a campaign to assert Crown authority west of the Shannon. The first fort was begun in 1269 by the justiciar Robert de Uffort, but this was demolished by the native Irish under Hugh O'Connor in 1272 and again in 1277. After this failure, the justiciary in the early 1280s embarked on a stronger, more impregnable fortress, built to the latest military specifications. Similar to Harlech Castle, which it predated by three years, this castle comprised a large quadrangle with projecting D-shaped corner towers and an unusually fine twin-towered gatehouse in the centre of the east wall. A rectangular tower with a postern gate projects from the west curtain close to the south-west tower; nearby stood the hall. A moat with drawbridges surrounded the castle at some distance from the walls, presumably filled from a lake that formerly lay close by.

Roscommon Castle

The castle was stormed in 1308 by a local chief, Donogh O'Kelly, and most of the inhabitants were slain. It remained in Irish hands, though probably largely deserted, until recovered by Sir Henry Sidney from the O'Connors in 1569. Nine years later it was granted to the Governor of Connaught, Sir Nicholas Malby, who built a splendid manor house on the east and north sides of the courtyard, with large mullioned windows inserted into the old walls. This appears to have had gardens on the east side enclosed by high walls with bastions. From 1645 to 1652 the castle was occupied by Confederate Catholics, but was dismantled after surrendering to the Cromwellians.

Located on NW side of the town off the Tulsk Road (N61). Access down a lane and over a stile on the right. NGR: M 874649. National Monument. The caretaker is Joe Leyden, Creevy; tel: (0903) 262209.

BALLINAFAD CASTLE
County Sligo

This neat little castle was built as a government military post by Captain St Barbe around 1590 to defend an important pass through the Curlew Mountains, and hence is known as the Castle of the Curlews. It comprises an oblong block of three storeys over a raised basement with stout towers at the corners. There were square rooms in all the towers save the north, where there was a circular timber stair. The door at first-floor level was secured with a draw-bar and had an internal grille or gate.

In the early seventeenth century the castle was garrisoned by a constable and ten warders. In 1642 it was attacked by the insurgent Irish and its defenders were forced to surrender due to lack of water.

Located in the village 6 miles N of Boyle on the Sligo road (N4). Access up a path and over a stile. Signposted.
NGR: G 7808. National Monument. Keys from Bernard Mulhern, Ballinafad; tel: (079) 66009.

BALLYMOTE CASTLE
County Sligo

Ballymote, begun in 1300, was the last and the mightiest of the Norman castles in Connaught. It was built some distance from an earlier motte by Richard de Burgo, the great Red Earl of Ulster, in order to protect his newly won possessions in Sligo. Almost square in plan with massive three-quarter round towers at each angle, it is the most symmetrical of all the Irish "keepless" castles and bears an unmistakable resemblance to the inner ward of Beaumaris in Anglesea (begun 1295). There was a formidable double-towered gate in the centre of the north wall and subsidiary D-shaped towers in the centre of the east and west curtain walls. Recent excavations revealed that the gate towers, now largely demolished, were protected by a double skin of external walling. A postern gate planned for the centre of the south wall was never completed, probably because of the events of 1317, when the castle was lost to the O'Connors.

Possession of the castle from 1317 until 1584 alternated between the O'Connors and the MacDonaghs. A lack of occupation levels implies that the building was virtually abandoned during these years. In 1584 it was taken by the notorious governor of Connaught, Richard Bingham, and remained an English base until lost to Red Hugh O'Donnell in 1598. It was here that O'Donnell assembled his forces on route to Kinsale in 1601. In 1652 the castle was surrendered by the Taaffes to parliamentary forces, and in 1690 it was captured by the Williamites, who soon afterwards had it dismantled and the moat filled in.

Located 15 miles S of Sligo at W end of Ballymote village. Access through St John of God's Nursing Home. NGR: G 660154. National Monument.

BALLYNAHOW CASTLE
County Tipperary

There is something rather attractive about round tower houses, but sadly only a relatively small number were built, mostly in Munster. Perhaps the finest to survive is the impressive early sixteenth-century tower of the Purcells at Ballynahow. It stands five storeys high with two internal vaults, each covering two storeys; the top storey was formerly covered by a conical timber roof carried on squinch arches. Both the lower floors were dimly lit round chambers that were probably used for storage, though their size was relatively small because of the wall's thickness at this level. The three storeys above were larger and approximated to a rectangular shape, with ogival and segmental-headed windows. One of the thicker segments of the wall was cleverly used to contain the entrance porch with its murder hole, the winding stair, the latrines and a number of other mural chambers. A number of small musket holes can be found near some of the principal windows.

Ballynahow Castle

Located 3 miles W of Thurles, off the Ballycahill road
(T19). Approached down a private avenue. NGR: S 082602.
National Monument. Open access. The caretaker,
James Finn, runs a bed and breakfast in the farmyard;
tel: (0504) 21297.

BURNTCOURT CASTLE

County Tipperary

The magnificent shell of this great seventeenth-century
embattled house derives its peculiar name from being burnt
by the Parliamentary army on their march to Cahir in
January 1650. Cromwell himself mentions stopping at the
"stronghouse called Clogheen, belonging to Sir Richard
Everard", though there is a tradition that the chatelaine,
Lady Everard, set fire to it prior to his arrival. This gave
rise to an old rhyme saying, "It was seven years in building,
seven years in living and fifteen days in burning". Sir
Richard Everard – a distinguished Catholic Royalist and
leading member of the Kilkenny Confederation – was
hanged by Ireton in 1651, and his castle, quaintly referred
to as "Burnt-Clogheen" in an inquisition of 1693, was
never rebuilt.

The stronghouse was erected on lands granted to Sir
Richard Everard by Charles I in 1639. A datestone recording the building's completion in 1641 was once placed over
one of the doors, but now is inserted in the wall at the entrance to the nearby farmyard. That year Sir Richard and
his family left their old ancestral castle at Ballyboy to take
up residence at their splendid new home five miles distant.
Known at the time as Clogheen, it was one of the largest
private dwellings then built in Ireland and comprised a
centre block of two storeys over a raised basement with a
gabled attic and four gabled corner towers – the whole
building having no less than twenty-six gables. The large
number of regularly disposed two-and three-mullioned
windows, all crowned by square-ended hood-mouldings,
gives the building a quiet, residential air, but its basic
design is defensive, notably the use of corner towers, which
permits flanking fire along each face of the house. Indeed,
the building has numerous firing-holes, while the projecting
corbels on the back and front supported a timber guard-
walk between the towers, which no doubt also served as a
machicolation. There are pistol loops in the jambs of the
back door opening out of the kitchen in the south end, and
also in the front entrance on the west side, which also has

a nicely cut hood moulding with celtic motifs around it, very similar to Monkstown Castle, County Cork.

During the eighteenth century an artist, Anthony Chearnley (*fl.* 1740-85), built a two-storey, five-bay gable-ended house in the bawn and laid out formal gardens outside the bawn wall. A number of engravings, based on drawings by him of Burntcourt *c.* 1759, show the ruins as they are now, except that the chimney-stacks were then complete.

Located 8.5 miles SW of Caher and 4 miles NE of Ballyporeen. Access through a farmyard and over a field. NGR: R 951181. National Monument.

CAHIR CASTLE

County Tipperary

Superbly set on a rocky island in the River Suir, this impressive fifteenth-century castle — the largest of its period in Ireland — was considered impregnable until the advent of heavy cannon. Described by one Elizabethan commentator as "the bulwark for Munster and a safe retreat for all the agents of Spain and Rome", it fell to Devereux, Earl of Essex, in 1599 after it had been battered for two days with artillery. It surrendered without a fight to Inchiquin in 1647 and again to Cromwell in 1650, but otherwise had a notably undistinguished history, which possibly helps to explain why it survives in such remarkably good condition today.

Making excellent use of the rocky terrain, its layout comprised a series of courts — an inner, middle, outer and barbican — which cleverly served as a successive line of defence, so that each ward or court dominated the one outside. The core of the castle, the inner ward, lies at the north end on the highest part of the island. It is surrounded by very thick curtain walls, the lowest parts of which belong to the original fortress on the site that was built by Philip of Worcester in the thirteenth century, after he moved here from the motte at Knockgraffron, three miles north. The massive wall-footing across the middle ward marks the south perimeter of this early castle, while the large adjacent building, known as the keep, originally served as the gatehouse, with a passage through the centre flanked by guard chambers. After this was converted into the main residential block of the castle in the fifteenth century, the gate was moved alongside, possibly with its original arch. The double machicolation over this entrance is largely an 1840s reconstruction, but the adjacent round tower, which served as a prison, may also have thirteenth-century foundations.

The present castle appears to be largely the work of Seamus Gallda (James the Foreigner), ancestor of the Butlers, Barons of Cahir. After the death of his father, the

Cahir Castle

third Earl of Ormonde, in 1405, James Butler made Cahir his principal seat and embarked on a building programme. This work was continued by his successors during the fifteenth and sixteenth centuries. By 1599 the castle had reached its present appearance when illustrated in *Pacata Hibernia*. The only subsequent alterations took place in the 1840s when Richard Butler, the thirteenth Baron Cahir, restored the castle and replaced the picturesque Irish battlements with more solid English ones. The great hall on the east side of the inner ward was also rebuilt at this time, though its original form extended much further south; indeed, the main fireplace now lies outside in the open.

The Butlers ceased to occupy the castle in the eighteenth century and built a house in the town, now the Cahir House Hotel. In the 1860s they erected a mansion, Cahir Park, in the magnificent parkland which adjoins the old castle.

> Located in the town. Access is through a modern gateway from the road bridge. NGR: S 048248. National Monument. Open daily April to mid-June: 10.00 am – 6.00 pm. Mid-June to mid-September: 9.00 am – 7.30 pm. Mid-September to mid-October: 10.00 am – 6.00 pm. Mid-October to March: 10.00 am – 4.30 pm. Closed during 1.00 – 2.00 pm from mid-October to March. Admission fee charged. Guided tours on request. Tel: (052) 41011.

CARRICK-ON-SUIR CASTLE
County Tipperary

This castle of the Butlers – Earls and later Dukes of Ormonde – stands above the Suir on the east side of Carrick. It was acquired in 1315, though the oldest part of the castle is a mid-fifteenth-century walled bawn with a tower house in each of its northern corners. Sometime after 1565 the tenth, or "Black", Earl of Ormonde, who spent many years in the court of his cousin Queen Elizabeth I, added a Tudor manor house of a type common in England but like no other in Ireland. The low U-shaped range of this house forms three sides of a small court attached to the north of the old bawn, whose towers rise behind it. It has two storeys with a gabled attic, rows of mullioned windows with curved-headed lights, and steep brick gables with slender finials. There are few defensive features save for small firing-holes either side of the front door.

The house was a favourite haunt of the Great Duke of Ormonde, but afterwards it was deserted by the family, although they continued to own it until the present century. Fortunately, it was never allowed to fall into complete ruin and in 1947 was taken over by the State, who subsequently conserved the building. Their most notable achievement was the restoration of the long gallery on the first floor of the front elevation, whose ceiling had largely collapsed.

This delightful room, once hung with tapestries, has a magnificent limestone mantel bearing the date 1565, and stucco representations of Queen Elizabeth flanked by Equity and Justice. The Queen would have felt at home in this room and in the rest of this house, which was probably intended, for she is believed to have promised her favourite cousin "Black Tom" that she would one day honour Carrick with a visit.

Located by the river at E end of Castle Street in remains of a park. NGR: S 405216. State Care Monument. Open daily mid-June to September: 9.30 am – 6.30 pm. Last admission 45 minutes before closing. Admission fee charged. Tel: Michael Wallace, 7 Greenhill Close, Pill Road on (051) 40787.

NENAGH CASTLE
County Tipperary

The finest cylindrical keep in Ireland – known to generations of Tipperary people as the "Nenagh Round" – was built around 1200 by Theobald Walter, the founder of the great Butler dynasty of Ormonde. It formed the north corner of a pentagonal court with a towered gatehouse on the southern side and strong towers on the north-west and south-east angles. This has now vanished, save for fragments of the gatehouse and east tower, but the keep survives to a height of 100 feet. Its topmost quarter was added about 1860 by the Catholic Bishop of Killaloe in emulation of Windsor Castle – the original height to the wall-walk being about 75 feet. There were four storeys, including a basement, with a first-floor entrance giving access to a winding mural stair that was once enclosed by a protecting turret. The second and third floors have narrow loops with large embrasures for cross-bowmen, but the top floor is well lit by four windows and was clearly the main chamber. It has a fireplace with early Gothic decoration, behind which there is a projecting machicoulis that protected a door leading from the floor below onto the curtain wall.

The Butlers remained at Nenagh until the mid-fourteenth-century, when they moved to Gowran and later purchased Kilkenny Castle in 1391. During the fifteenth century it was occupied by the O'Briens, but was recovered in 1533 by Sir Piers Ruadh Butler, later Earl of Ormonde. The castle changed hands many times before and during the Cromwellian wars, but after its capture by Ginkel in 1690, the place was dismantled by the Williamites. The Butler link was finally broken in 1703 when the second Duke of Ormonde sold the property to pay debts.

Located between O'Rahilly Street and St Flannan Street, through the grounds of the Catholic church. NGR: R 865794. National Monument. Key with Liam White, 4 O'Rahilly Street.

BENBURB CASTLE
County Tyrone

The name Benburb, roughly translated as "proud peak", aptly describes the setting of this Plantation bawn, perched on the summit of a limestone cliff towering 200 feet above the River Blackwater. It was built in 1611-14 by an English servitor, Sir Richard Wingfield (later Viscount Powerscourt), who was granted 1,000 acres here from James I. An earlier castle on or close to the site was the "chief seat" of the celebrated Shane O'Neill, before it was burnt in 1566.

The bawn occupies a large irregular quadrangular area enclosed by walls standing almost to full height and generously fitted with musketry loop-holes. No main house was built as Wingfield had no desire to live here, but living accommodation was provided in gabled two-and-a-half storey rectangular flankers incorporated into the north-west and north-east corners of the bawn. One of these was occupied in 1622 by "Mr Moore, an Englishman, with his wife and family". In the south-east corner of the enclosure is a round stair turret giving access to a postern down the cliff, while the house on the south-west side was built in the late eighteenth century and remodelled in Victorian times.

The castle was captured on an October night in 1641 by Phelim O'Neill, who had all the inmates put to death. In 1646 it was occupied by Owen Roe O'Neill before he defeated the English army at the battle of Benburb. It was dismantled soon afterwards and has remained a ruin ever since.

Located S of the village main street in the grounds of Benburb Servite Priory. NGR: H 814520. State Care Monument. Open public access.

CASTLE CAULFIELD
County Tyrone

Sir Toby Caulfield, later Lord Charlemont (1565-1627), must have had a very strong desire to live like an English gentleman, for he was prepared to build an unfortified English-style mansion in an unsettled area of Ulster during the period 1611-19. Described by Pynnar in 1619 as "the fairest building in the north", it had three storeys with attics in a U-shaped plan – the north-west wing of which has now disappeared. It had fireplaces in projecting breasts and massive chimney stacks capped with octagonal stone shafts, as well as flat-headed mullioned and transomed windows, most of which have been torn out. The gatehouse, with its vaulted passage and guard chambers, probably belong to an earlier O'Donnelly bawn on the site.

During the 1641 Rebellion the house was burnt by Patrick "the Gloomy" O'Donnelly and some of the interior stonework still shows signs of scorching. In the 1660s the house was partially rehabilitated by the Caulfields, who were in residence in 1670 when Archbishop Oliver Plunket was permitted to use the courtyard for ordinations. It was probably disused by 1700 and was a ruin when John Wesley preached in front of the gates in 1767.

Located on the SE edge of Castlecaulfield village opposite a housing estate. NGR: H 755626. State Care Monument. Open public access.

HARRY AVERY'S CASTLE
County Tyrone

A curiously enigmatic castle named after and possibly built by Henry Aimbreidh O'Neill, a Gaelic chief celebrated by the Four Masters for his justice, nobility and hospitality, who died in 1392. The castle commands wide views over the Mourne Valley and is unusual in being a stone-built stronghold located deep in the heart of pre-Plantation Ulster. It consists of a two-storey rectangular block fronted by a pair of massive D-shaped towers – resembling a gatehouse – projecting from the south face of an artificially scarped knoll, whose sides have been revetted by a wall to form a polygonal enclosure, now ruined to a low level with traces of a latrine tower on the north side. Excavations in 1950 and 1962 confirmed that the keep-like structure functioned more as a tower house than as a true gatehouse, though the only access into the enclosure behind seems to have been up a narrow mural stair and through the hall at first-floor level. The entrance has a draw-bar

Harry Avery's Castle

slot, while other features include vaults with traces of wickercentering and latrine shafts in one of the towers.

The castle was captured by the English in 1609. Subsequently, it was used as a quarry for building material.

Located three-quarters of a mile SW of Newtownstewart in a field off the Rakelly road. NGR: H 323852. State Care Monument. Open access.

ATHLONE CASTLE

County Westmeath

Athlone used to be one of the most formidable medieval fortresses in Ireland, but warfare and substantial rebuilding have left little of the old castle above internal ground level. The construction of both a bridge and castle at this key river crossing began in 1210, following King John's visit to Ireland, when the justiciar, Bishop Henry de Grey, was ordered to begin settling the middle Shannon region between Meath and Connaught. De Grey's stone tower, probably built on an earlier motte of 1199, had to be rebuilt the following year after it collapsed, killing nine of the garrison. It was again repaired in 1251 and in 1273-79 the curtain walls were probably added, flanked by massive D-shaped towers. Most of this structure was still present when drawn by Thomas Phillips in 1685, together with a fine suite of apartments, used by the Lord President of Connaught, overlooking the river on the east side.

The castle's strategic position meant that it saw a good deal of military action. In 1691 it suffered the heaviest bombardment in Irish history when the Williamite General Ginkell battered it with over 600 bombs, 12,000 canon balls and huge quantities of stones from fifty-eight pieces of ordnance. From 1793 to 1815 the whole castle was rebuilt, reduced in height and strengthened for the mounting of heavy cannon in efforts to fortify the Shannon against French invasion. The lower storey of De Grey's polygonal tower is the only part of the medieval fabric to survive.

Located in the town. NGR: N 038413. National Monument. Open daily May to September: 10.00 am – 4.30 pm (last tour 4.30 pm). Admission fee charged. Visitor centre with military exhibition and audio-visual presentation of the 1691 siege. A local museum founded by the Old Athlone Society is housed in the tower. Tel: (0902) 92912.

ENNISCORTHY CASTLE
County Wexford

The town of Enniscorthy developed around this much rebuilt and restored thirteenth-century castle standing on a rock at the head of the Slaney's navigable tideway. The original building was probably built by Gerald de Prendergast during the 1230s, and like both Ferns and Carlow, comprised a rectangular keep of four storeys strengthened at the corners by communicating three-quarter drum towers. In 1253 it passed through marriage to the Rochford family, and by the early fifteenth century was held by the MacMurrough Kavanaghs. By the 1530s the castle was evidently in Crown possession and serving as the Seneschal's residence. It was leased to Edmund Spencer for three days in 1581 and five years later was acquired by Sir Henry Wallop, who refortified the building and resided there occasionally until 1597. It was captured by

Cromwellian troops in 1649 and was used as a prison during the 1798 Rebellion.

During the early nineteenth century the castle suffered a restoration by the Earl of Plymouth, and yet another at the end of the century by a local MP who enlarged it and used it as a residence. The building now houses a museum.

Located within the town. NGR: S 971399. Now the County Museum. Open June to September: 10.00 am – 9.00 pm. October to May: 2.00 – 5.00 pm. Admission fee charged.

FERNS CASTLE
County Wexford

The much-ruined castle at Ferns is the largest of a distinctive group of thirteenth-century Hiberno-Norman keeps that comprise rectangular blocks with cylindrical corner towers. Known as "towered" or "four-towered" keeps, they evolved independently in the South Leinster region at least a century before any comparable castles were built in England. Considering the great size of the Ferns keep it is perhaps surprising that we have no historical reference for the date of its building, but it was probably begun around 1222 by Earl William Marshall the younger. Architectural details, however, suggest that it was not completed until the mid-thirteenth-century, when it was held by William de Valance, husband of a Marshall heiress.

In its heyday the castle must have been particularly imposing. The three storeys of the main block were divided by partitions into vast apartments, the upper floors of which were lit by rather splendid trefoil-pointed windows, mostly grouped in pairs beneath pointed and camber-headed embrasures. There are similar windows in the beautiful circular chapel on the second floor of the largely complete south-east tower. This room, often cited as the most perfect chapel to be found in any Irish castle, is particularly noteworthy for its moulded rib-vaulting and supporting corbels in the shape of capitals. Of the other corner towers, one has vanished, only fragments remain of another, while about half survives of the south-west tower, which has a cellar hollowed out of solid rock, said to have been used to keep Kathleen, daughter of William Marshall, to prevent her eloping. Outside the walls a rock-cut ditch was partly re-exposed during archaeological excavations carried out by David Sweetman in 1972-75. A draw-bridge structure on the south side was also revealed and another possible entrance on the east side.

The castle evidently ceased being a residence in the early fourteenth century, for the ditch appears to have been filled by about 1310, while the building was in a bad state of repair by 1324. It was captured by the O'Tooles in 1331, recovered by Bishop Charnell shortly afterwards, and seems to have stayed in the hands of the Bishopric of Ferns until the 1370s when it was taken by the MacMurroughs. Lord Grey captured the place during the 1536 revolt, but the MacMurroughs managed to remain until 1551, when it was taken over for the Crown by John Travers. The Mastersons held the castle from 1583 until 1649, when it was surrendered to Cromwellian soldiers. It is likely these troops were responsible for demolishing much of its structure.

Located at NW end of village. NGR: T 017501. National Monument. Caretaker Jim Gethings, 36 Castle View, Ferns.

RATHMACKNEE CASTLE

County Wexford

Many Irish castles have lost their parapets during the course of time, but those at Rathmacknee are fully intact and are a superb example of the picturesque multi-stepped

Rathmacknee Castle

crenellations so characteristic of late medieval Irish architecture. Other features of the castle have survived equally well, and although now lacking its roof and floors, it may be considered one of the most complete examples of a tower house in South Leinster.

The tower occupies the south-east corner of a well-preserved five-sided bawn that has a boldy projecting machicolation above the entrance. In plan the tower is a simple rectangle with one small projection – a prolongation southwards in the east wall to accommodate latrines. There is a mural stair linking all five storeys, each having one apartment with closets or chambers in the thickness of the wall. The two lower storeys are beneath vaulting, while the timber floors had cross beams that were tenoned directly into the wall beams rather than laid directly upon them – an unusual practice that allowed the depth of the floor to be reduced.

It is probable that the castle was built by John Rossiter, Seneschal of the Liberties of Wexford in 1451, whose family had lived in this area since the late twelfth century. Though staunch Catholics, they survived the Reformation purges, but ultimately forfeited their lands in the 1650s. The castle remained occupied until the 1760s.

Located 7.5 miles SW of Wexford town, lying down a lane, off a minor road, due W of the main Kilmore road. Signposted. NGR: T 037143. National Monument. Key obtainable from Patrick Kavanagh in the modern house situated in the bawn.

SLADE CASTLE
County Wexford

The picturesque little harbour of Slade is dominated by the brown rubble walls and striking merlons of this castle, formerly home of the Laffans – possibly merchants here in late medieval times. The building comprises a tower house built in the late fifteenth or early sixteenth century, and an attached two-storey hall of slightly later date.

The tower, standing 56 feet high and gracefully tapered, contains a mural stair in the south-east angle and barrel vaults over the second and fifth floors; above the latter rises a turret accommodating the stair head, a small apartment and the base of what was once a tall chimney-stack. The rooms were all very small, including the main chamber on the third floor, which had a latrine, fireplace, cupboard recess and two windows. No doubt the two-storey house was later added to provide more living space, though it was built as a separate unit at an obtuse angle to the tower. It has its own entrance on the south side, leading via a lobby up a straight mural staircase to three fair-sized rooms on the first floor. A low-pitched slated roof once covered these rooms rising from the wall-walk behind the attractive many-stepped battlemented parapet, though on the east side the roof was at a higher level to accommodate an extra storey. The three ground-floor rooms – all with heavy pointed vaults – strangely cannot be entered from the living quarters above and may have always been intended as a warehouse on the quay.

The castle was forfeited by the Laffan family in the aftermath of the 1641 Rebellion, though the Laffan heir was only a young boy who could not possibly have been implicated in the war. The building appears to have been used and extended in the late eighteenth century as part of an extensive salt works adjoining the site.

Located at the E end of Hook Head, 6 miles SW of Fethard-on-Sea. NGR: X 747986. National Monument. Key obtainable from Richard Rice, Slade House; tel: (051) 97155.

INDEX OF CASTLES